Guide to OSF/1: *A Technical Synopsis*

Books That Help People
Get More Out of Computers

UNIX for FORTRAN Programmers, 264 pages
By Mike Loukides

This handbook minimizes the UNIX entry barrier, by providing the serious scientific programmer with an introduction to the UNIX operating system and its tools.

Programming Perl, 482 pages
By Larry Wall & Randal Schwartz

Authoritative guide to the hottest new UNIX utility in years, co-authored by the creator of that utility. Perl is a language for easily manipulating text, files and processes.

lex & yacc, 238 pages
By Tony Mason & Doug Brown

Complete guide to using two UNIX utilities, *lex* and *yacc*, to solve problems in program development.

sed & awk, 414 pages
By Dale Dougherty

For people who create and modify text files, *sed* and *awk* are power tools for editing. Most of the things that you can do with these programs can be done interactively with a text editor. However, using *sed* and *awk* can save many hours of repetitive work in achieving the same result.

Power Programming with RPC, 500 pages~
By John Bloomer

RPC or remote procedure calling is the ability to distribute the execution of functions on remote computers. Written from a programmer's perspective, this book shows what you can do with RPC and presents a framework for learning it.

The X Window System Series

These nine volumes are the definitive guides to the X Window System and include complete manuals on the X Protocol, Xlib programming, Xlib reference, X Toolkit Intrinsics programming and reference, Motif programming, and XView programming. A user guide and desktop quick-reference fill out the series.

Contact us for a catalog of our books, for orders, or for more information.

O'Reilly & Associates, Inc.

632 Petaluma Avenue, Sebastopol CA 95472
(800) 338-6887 US/Canada   707-829-0515 overseas/local   707-829-0104 Fax

Guide to OSF/1:
A Technical Synopsis

O'Reilly & Associates, Inc.
632 Petaluma Avenue
Sebastopol, CA 95472

Guide to OSF/1: A Technical Synopsis

Copyright © 1991 O'Reilly & Associates, Inc.
All rights reserved.

Printed in the United States of America

Printing History

June 1991:   First printing.

TABLE OF CONTENTS

PREFACE

This book contains no attempt at the comparative analysis of operating systems or the critical assessment of OSF/1's strengths and weaknesses. It is rather intended to fill an immediate need for information: what *is* OSF/1? How is it being described by the people who developed it, and what promises and commitments for its future are being made by those people? We have attempted, as far as possible, to present the Open Software Foundation's own view of OSF/1, without interposing commentary of our own. In the rather politicized and competitive world of UNIX standards, there is value in allowing the major players to speak as clearly as possible, for all to hear and evaluate. We hope this book may become the first of several featuring some of the newer and often controversial efforts to establish software standards.

The book is rooted in a training seminar licensed from OSF. This material originally consisted of slides with minimal commentary, and we have chosen to retain the same look and feel. Each one- or two-page section begins with a slide-like illustration, followed by brief comments designed to be relatively self-contained. Though we have at times slipped into a somewhat more connected and extended narrative than is customary with slide presentations, the material remains largely sentential, abbreviated, suggestive, and sometimes slightly disconnected. And while we occasionally find ourselves thinking that this is exactly the way the high-tech world likes to consume its information, we're not at all sure we ourselves feel comfortable with it. Perhaps you will let us know your own reactions.

All of which is to say that this book is not your usual O'Reilly and Associates Nutshell Handbook or X Windows manual. It is an experiment.

Strengths and limitations of the presentation

We offer here a technical synopsis. That means two things. First, it is indeed a synopsis, or *overview*; you will not find here a detailed exposition of operating system internals or design, such as you would want if you were beginning to port OSF/1 to a new platform. Second, the descriptions are, however, *technical*. They assume that you are already at least minimally familiar with the UNIX operating system and with general computing concepts and terminology.

With those caveats, let us tell you what we think the book does well. It gives you a good feel for the overall character of the OSF/1 operating system and explains a broad range of its distinctive features. It relates many of these features to traditional UNIX implementations, suggesting wherever possible why changes were desirable. It defines buzzwords and practices that are emerging in association with newer operating systems. And, perhaps most importantly, it serves as a tutorial, gently leading the non-specialist into a significant first acquaintance with extensible loaders and shared libraries, lazy evaluation and memory objects, POSIX threads and Mach messages.

This last deserves emphasis. While we said the book is technical, it is also true that it assumes as little as possible. We would like to think that—quite apart from its educational value with respect to a particular operating system—it is worth its asking price as a general introduction to some of those features soon to be commonplace in modern operating systems.

One other attraction: we have observed extraordinary levels of interest in the forthcoming Distributed Computing Environment (DCE), due for its initial release from OSF in the Fall of 1991. But despite the interest, specific knowledge about the content of DCE is hard to come by. Considering the large number of companies that have "signed up" for this product, it is remarkable that so few people—even in those very companies—know just what it is they have signed up for. We have therefore included in this book a judicious "look ahead", sketching in significant detail the noteworthy features of DCE.

Finally, we have placed a premium upon the little-known and little-understood. That means, for example, that OSF/1 components such as STREAMS (from AT&T's System V, Release 3) and sockets (from Berkeley UNIX) do not receive treatment here, beyond occasional mention, while internationalization and security features are described at considerable length. STREAMS and sockets are, after all, adequately documented elsewhere. We have focused our own efforts on those parts of the operating system subject to the most intense curiosity and "need to know".

Comments and questions

Please address comments and questions to the publisher:

O'Reilly & Associates, Inc.
632 Petaluma Avenue
Sebastopol CA 95472
1-800-338-6887 (in US or Canada)
1-707-829-0515 (international/local)
1-707-829-0104 (FAX)

You can also send us messages electronically. To be put on the mailing list or request a catalog, send e-mail to:

nuts@ora.com (via the Internet)   or   uunet!ora!nuts (via UUCP)

To ask technical questions or comment on the book, send e-mail to:

bookquestions@ora.com (Internet)   or   uunet!ora!bookquestions (UUCP)

Acknowledgments

Our book is based, in the first place, upon the Open Software Foundation's "OSF/1 Technical Seminar". However, we have greatly revised virtually all of that material, and added large sections of our own. In addition, we reprint in appendices various documents from OSF that complement our presentation.

We owe thanks to the many co-workers at O'Reilly and Associates and Cambridge Computer Associates who made possible our fanatically short publication schedule (lasting one month from commencement of writing until delivery to the printer). Despite the inevitability of omissions, we would at least like to mention the following: Victor Oppenheimer, who first proposed the book to us, and who, together with his colleague, Bob Tinkelman, acted as a careful reviewer and also had a hand in the earlier preparation of the OSF/1 Technical Seminar; Debby Russell, for her assistance with the chapter on security; Mike Loukides, for his helpful comments on several of the chapters; Edie Freedman, who was always available for instant artistic advice, and who would have been responsible for numerous felicities of book design had our mad rush to the printer not forced us to compromise her suggestions—suggestions that remain, nevertheless, the source of all redeeming qualities in the book's appearance; Chris Reilly, who worked long hours to prepare the book's illustrations on short notice; and Sue Willing, for her valuable services as a proofreader. In addition, Al Lehotsky, Jim Van Sciver, and Bernice Moy of OSF gave us a crucial boost with their technical reviews of the book. And special thanks are also due to Elizabeth Connolly and Richard Martin of OSF, together with several of their colleagues.

Linda Mui   O'Reilly and Associates
Steve Talbott

1

OVERVIEW:
OSF and OSF/1

IN THIS CHAPTER

- Open systems
- The open process
- OSF offerings
- What is OSF/1?
- OSF advertises heavy reliance on standards
- What is Mach?

1.1

> "A truly open computing environment would employ a standard set of interfaces for programming, communications, networking, system management, and user 'look and feel', so software applications would become uncoupled from the platforms on which they run."
>
> – OSF

Open systems

OSF—the Open Software Foundation—presents itself as an advocate of "open systems". What does that mean? In OSF's own words, it means—

Portability. "Operating systems for open computing environments must adhere to industrywide standards and specifications for the interfaces they provide to system and applications software .... The operating system itself must be portable enough to be moved easily onto different classes of hardware—from personal computers to supercomputers".

Scalability. Portability between such a range of computing systems in turn "enables users to increase processing power as their business needs grow, without the need to re-write applications".

Interoperability. "In the diverse environment of open systems, each system must communicate and cooperate easily with its neighbors and associates whether they are in the same room or on the other side of the world. This is the open systems goal of interoperability".

Here's more from OSF on the subject of open systems:

"The Open Software Foundation was formed in May of 1988 specifically to develop core software technologies and supply them to the entire industry, on fair and reasonable terms. Although OSF is using established UNIX technology as the basis for its initial software development, its objective is not to develop the definitive version of the UNIX system.

"OSF's objective is to broaden the definition of openness in computing . . . . [A truly open computing] environment would not mean the elimination of proprietary operating systems. It would provide a point of connection to them, so that vendor lock-in could be avoided. Because applications could be purchased from any software vendor whose products were compatible with the application interface, independent software vendors would have an enormous incentive to provide more applications software".

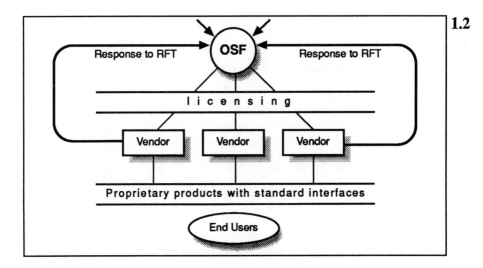

1.2

The open process

OSF has more than 200 members from among computer manufacturers, software development companies, commercial end users, research organizations, universities, and government agencies. Its charter is to bring together vendors, consumers, and researchers in a neutral setting, to discuss industry needs and to set the course for open systems.

Central to this process is the **Request for Technology**, or RFT. This is the means by which OSF solicits and evaluates technology from both members and non-member interested parties. In selecting particular technologies for its offerings, OSF takes into consideration the advice of its membership as well as the recommendations of industry consultants, standards groups, and non-member companies that have responded to the Requests for Technology.

Having evaluated and acquired relevant technology, OSF works to make a product out of it, consistent with the mandate to encourage the development of open systems. Such products are available without restriction to any individual or organization choosing to **license the rights**. (Over the long run, it is intended that OSF should support itself through the sale of licenses.) Note, however, that OSF is not in the business of selling end-user products. It licenses software to vendors who in turn port the software to their own hardware, or assimilate it into their own software, and then sell the resulting products to their customers.

While anyone may license OSF software, members are given the advantage of "early and equal access" by means of a "snapshot" program, whereby they receive (at a price) preliminary releases of specifications, software, and documentation currently under development. This allows vendors to do their porting and to develop their custom applications in parallel with the efforts at OSF.

1.3

- OSF/1 operating system
- Motif graphical user interface
- Distributed computing environment
- Architecture-neutral distribution format
- Distributed management environment

OSF offerings

Current and future offerings make up what OSF calls its "open computing environment". These offerings include:

OSF/1 operating system. This is intended to be a foundation for all the other offerings. However, the other offerings remain independent of OSF/1. For example, the distributed computing environment (DCE) can be—and is being—ported to System V, Release 4 UNIX from AT&T. Similarly, Motif has been ported to numerous operating systems other than OSF/1.

OSF/1 integrates software obtained from Carnegie Mellon University, Encore, IBM, Mentat, SecureWare, and the University of California. General availability of OSF/1 for licensing was announced in October, 1990.

Motif graphical user interface. Based on the X Window System developed at Massachusetts Institute of Technology, Motif lends a common look and feel to applications running on diverse machines ranging from personal computers to mainframes. It has attained wide distribution, having become available on more than 120 hardware platforms and 42 operating systems within one year of its July, 1989 release.

Distributed computing environment (DCE). In June, 1989, OSF issued a Request for Technology for a distributed computing environment. Submissions came in from 32 organizations. In May, 1990, the technology for DCE was selected, and the first "snapshot" of the offering was released in July, 1990. A remarkable array of organizations worldwide has endorsed the product.

The aim of DCE is to put the distributed resources of computer networks at the disposal of individual users and applications, without forcing those users and applications to understand the complexities of network implementation. In the latter part of this book (§13.1)[*] we provide a more extensive summary of DCE.

Architecture-neutral distribution format (ANDF). The intent here is to remove the need for porting applications to many different platforms. Applications can be written in a single, intermediate format, which is then convertible (by means of ANDF technology) for execution on specific platforms. An initial Request for Technology was issued in April, 1989, with a follow-up, "second-phase" request in February, 1990. As of this writing, no technology selection has been made.

Distributed management environment. "Through the distributed management environment Request for Technology, OSF will identify a uniform framework for the efficient, cost-effective management of open systems. That framework will support a wide range of diverse systems, from stand-alone to distributed". The Request for Technology was issued in July, 1990; as of this writing, the schedule calls for software selection in the Fall of 1991. See Appendix E for a brief OSF white paper outlining plans for the distributed management environment.

---

[*] Throughout this book we use the symbol § to signify a cross reference. The associated number matches a section number, as given alongside the top of each illustration.

1.4

- Mach Kernel
- Parallelized 4.4BSD UNIX
- S5, UFS, NFS file systems
- Logical volume manager
- Streams
- Extensible loader
- Dynamic configurability
- B-1 compliant security

What is OSF/1?

It is important to realize, first of all, that what OSF/1 turns out to be—what you discover in the computer at your fingertips—depends on the choices of your vendor. The operating system described in this book is the operating system that OSF licenses to vendors for porting to their separate platforms. What value those vendors choose to add—or remove—is not something we attempt to predict. Our aim is to describe "standard OSF/1", as released by its developers.

Many of the core (or "kernel") services provided by OSF/1 are derived from the **Mach operating system** (§1.6). Mach was designed from the ground up to support symmetric multiprocessing (parallel processing) and distributed computing. It also contains a native threads (§2.1) facility, allowing separate strands (threads) of a single application to execute simultaneously.

Mach was intended to be a relatively simple, extensible core, upon which other operating system services—interprocess communication, file systems, networking services, and security provisions—could be built. There are Mach implementations on many of today's major computer architectures.

Many of the more familiar UNIX features of OSF/1—layered on top of Mach—originate in the **4.3 BSD** and **4.4BSD** operating systems, developed at the University of California, Berkeley. However, the Berkeley code has been parallelized so as to take advantage of Mach parallel processing. All user and operating system activity can, with minor exceptions, run on multiple processors in parallel. (Signal handling mechanisms, along with a few other pieces, are not parallelized in the 1.0 release of OSF/1.)

OSF/1 supports **all major UNIX file systems**: the S5 file system of AT&T's System 5, the UFS file system of BSD UNIX, and the NFS file system of Sun Microsystems. The latter two have been parallelized. The NFS implementation was obtained, not from Sun, but from the University of Guelph, and is free of Sun NFS licensing.

The **logical volume manager** allows a single, logical file system—and even a single file—to span multiple physical "volumes". (A volume may be a disk drive, or some portion of a disk drive.) The logical volume manager supports disk mirroring, whereby every change to a file system is automatically mirrored by identical changes to one or two duplicate file systems on separate physical volumes. This provides reliability in the event of damage to a file system. It also makes possible some performance optimizations in file access.

OSF/1 includes a System V Release 3-compatible **STREAMS** package that has been parallelized, enabling existing STREAMS applications to take advantage of multiprocessing environments. STREAMS is a set of operating system facilities supporting character-based I/O. It can be used for implementing individual device drivers or extensive networking and communications packages.

The **extensible loader** allows multiple load formats, shared libraries, and run-time loading and unloading. Since modules can be loaded into the kernel dynamically, you can add device drivers, STREAMS modules, file systems, and communication protocols to a running system. This is **dynamic configurability**.

OSF/1 can be compiled for either **B1 or C2 security levels**, both of which draw upon technology from SecureWare. However, you have the option to stick with "traditional UNIX security" rather than use B1 or C2, if you wish. Indeed, this may be required if you want compatibility with existing applications.

1.5

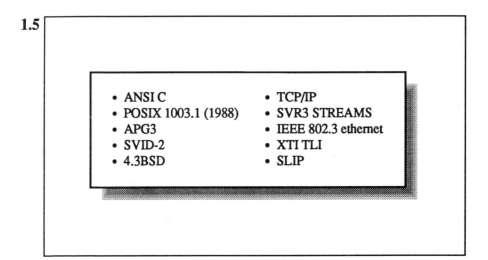

- ANSI C
- POSIX 1003.1 (1988)
- APG3
- SVID-2
- 4.3BSD

- TCP/IP
- SVR3 STREAMS
- IEEE 802.3 ethernet
- XTI TLI
- SLIP

OSF advertises heavy reliance on standards

OSF/1 conforms to the POSIX 1003.1-1988 standard. In those cases where POSIX allows alternatives, OSF/1 selects the alternative specified by FIPS 151-1 for government-purchased computing systems. OSF/1 also adheres to the X/Open Portability Guide Issue 3 (XPG3). OSF has promised to comply with XPG4 when it is published. In addition, OSF/1 supports elements of the IEEE draft POSIX 1003.4 specification, including portions relating to timers. OSF/1 threads conform to POSIX 1003.4a. All commands and libraries of the operating system are written in ANSI C.

OSF/1 is compatible with the base and kernel extensions of the System V Interface Definition (SVID), Issue 2, which corresponds to AT&T's System V, Release 3 of UNIX. Also, it is compatible with 4.3BSD applications. Since 4.4BSD was a base for the OSF/1 development effort, much of that code relating to processes, file systems, terminals, and sockets is intact; changes were made primarily for integration with Mach and for parallelization.

In the networking arena, OSF/1 includes parallelized versions of the TCP/IP Internet protocols; the BSD socket interface; System V, Release 3-compatible STREAMS support; an NFS-compatible file system; IEEE 802.3 ethernet protocol; Serial Line Interface Protocol (SLIP); and a parallelized X/Open Transport Interface (XTI), providing backward compatibility with AT&T's Transport Layer Interface (TLI).

OSF supplies three "reference implementations" on its release tape: one for an Intel 80386 (CISC) platform, one for the DECstation-3100 MIPS-based machine (RISC), and one for Encore's multiprocessor superminicomputer (National Semi-conductor 32532 chip). Three vendors have contributed ports of OSF/1, also on the tape: Hewlett-Packard, for the Motorola 68030 chip; Intergraph, for a Fairchild Clipper chip; and Intel for its own i860 chip.

1.6

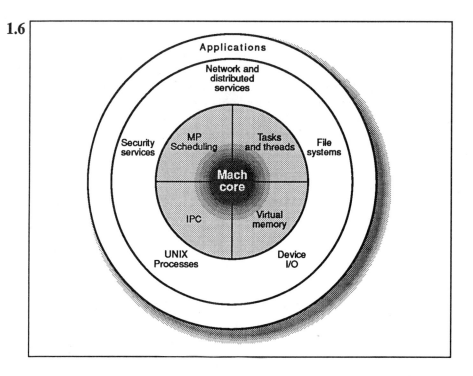

What is Mach?

Originally developed at Carnegie Mellon University, Mach has been modified and refined over the past six years under the auspices of the U.S. Defense Advanced Research Projects Agency (DARPA), with contributions from other research and commercial organizations. Today, thousands of Mach-based systems have been shipped by commercial suppliers, including NeXt, Encore, and Sequent.

Why Mach? The need for Mach is usually explained as resulting from two ongoing changes in computing:

- the advent of new computer architectures—particularly those employing multiple processors

- deficiencies in the UNIX operating system—particularly when implemented on the new architectures

Here is what some of the Mach developers have had to say about UNIX.

What was originally good about UNIX:

- simple programming interface

- largely portable to wide class of uniprocessors

- extensive utility program library

- easy to combine utilities

What went wrong with UNIX:

- the "kitchen sink" operating system became a dumping ground for every conceivable feature, good and bad

- the existing primitives were not well adapted for multiprocessing, with its requirement for memory sharing and "lightweight processes" (§2.1)

- these primitives were also inadequate for distributed computing, with its complex security requirements

- these same primitives were not fully up to supporting shared libraries, with their requirement for shared address spaces

- the operating system relied on too many "fundamental" abstractions

Mach development began as an effort to replace 4.3BSD UNIX with a better, though fully compatible, operating system. The compatibility remains, but the development effort led in many new directions. Key features of Mach include:

Support for symmetric multiprocessing. When multiple processors are present, any available processor can run any thread. (A thread is a single, executable "thread of control" in an executing program.) Fine-grained locking mechanisms ensure that a processor locks only the small portion of data that it needs, allowing other processors access to the remaining data. Programs can, if they choose, bind particular threads to particular processors. A multi-threaded program, even though originally written on a uniprocessor, can, without modification, take advantage of additional processors if they are available.

Support for interprocess communication. Mach provides low-level mechanisms for processes and threads to communicate with one another. These mechanisms include security features; unlike with UNIX sockets, the rights to communicate through particular channels are carefully controlled. The mechanisms are also location-independent: the sender need not know the address or location of the receiver, but can use certain generic, global names instead.

Mach-based virtual memory system. Whereas traditional UNIX virtual memory systems grew up on top of existing UNIX kernels, Mach virtual memory was designed from scratch, with maximum hardware independence. Features include copy-on-write, map-on-reference, and other applications of the principle of lazy evaluation (§4.2).

Easy portability. Mach cleanly distinguishes between the machine-dependent and machine-independent aspects of the operating system. Porting Mach to a new computer is therefore simplified, because only a relatively small component needs to be re-written for the new hardware.

Finally, OSF has declared its intention to move an increasing number of non-Mach (that is, non-core) functions **from the system to the user side** of the ledger. By this is meant that these functions will execute in "user space"—subject to user control—rather than in the more privileged and tightly controlled "system space". There are several advantages of flexibility and control in this policy:

- High-performance or specialized applications can tailor "operating system" functions to their own needs. For example, a user-written memory manager (already supported in release 1.0) might automatically encrypt/decrypt all data written to and read from a file system, for use in conjunction with a special, high-security application.

- Whereas errors in operating system code can crash the whole system, errors in user code more typically just crash the application.

- There are many more debugging tools for user programs than for operating system code.

Similarly, OSF/1 allows execution scheduling policies to be set by a user-level **processor server**. System administrators can change this server program and re-install it just like they would change any other user program, effectively re-configuring the operating system.

2

OSF/1 Architecture:

Tasks, Threads, and Processes

IN THIS CHAPTER

- Processes are the traditional units of execution under UNIX

- UNIX processes map closely to Mach tasks

- OSF/1 process data structures differ from traditional UNIX

- OSF/1 allows you to match threads with processors

- Dispatching threads for execution

- Messages and memory are closely related in OSF/1

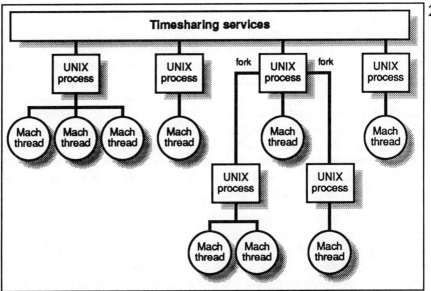

2.1

Processes are the traditional units of execution under UNIX

If you write a program and compile it on a traditional, single-processor UNIX system, that program runs as a single process. You can think of the process as a *virtual computer*: it consists of a set of instructions running sequentially on the CPU, and associated with it are input and output devices, its own memory, and various system resources used by the operating system to identify, schedule, prioritize, and manage the execution of the process.

On uniprocessor **timesharing systems,** many such processes may appear to be running at the same time. The fact is, however, that this is only an appearance. Actually, there is never more than one process executing on the single CPU; the operating system achieves the "simultaneous" feel by time-slicing the various processes—switching between them so rapidly that, under favorable conditions, each process seems to be executing continuously.

UNIX allows processes to **fork,** or split up, so that a single program can consist of several processes, each enjoying its own slices of the computer's time—that is, each constituting a virtual computer. When a process splits in this way, all the resources belonging to the original, or parent, process are typically duplicated. This means, for example, that the entire memory space of the parent is duplicated for the child.

Mach introduces the idea of a **thread**, as in "thread of control". Threads—sometimes called lightweight processes—can also be thought of as virtual computers, inasmuch as they comprise sequences of instructions together with system resources such as memory. However, those resources are, to a substantial degree, shared among all the threads within a process. A process can create a thread much as it spawns a child process, except that not all the parent's resources are duplicated for each thread. Threads are therefore quick and easy to create, while offering the same potential for multiple virtual computers as processes do. (It has been estimated that creating a thread takes about 1/10th the time of a UNIX *fork/exec* combination.) On the other hand, because of the shared resources, they require closer coordination than companion processes do; for where resources are shared, they may also be used in conflicting ways.

On a computer with more than one CPU, both processes and threads offer a potential for **parallelism**: multiple processes or threads can execute in true simultaneity, one per CPU. Furthermore, realizing this potential need not require re-writing applications. Since threads and processes can run in time-sliced fashion on uniprocessor machines, you can write your application so as to utilize such multiple strands of control, and they will work in either uniprocessor or multiprocessor environments, profiting greatly from the increased performance of the latter. When threads run on separate CPUs, they continue to share the virtual memory of the parent process (§4.1).

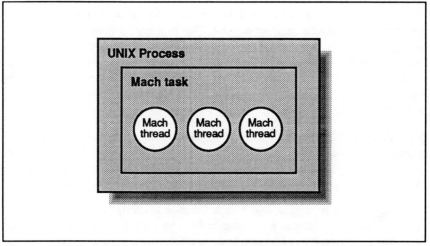

UNIX processes map closely to Mach tasks

The Mach core of OSF/1 implements threads and tasks. We haven't spoken yet of **tasks**, which correspond fairly closely to UNIX processes. However, a task is not an executable entity. It is simply a holder of system resources—the sort of resources that processes require, such as memory, communication channels, and identification and priority information.

It is easiest to grasp what a task is by thinking in terms of **UNIX processes**. In OSF/1 a traditional UNIX, non-multi-threaded process is implemented as a single Mach thread operating in the resource context of a single Mach task. Or, again: the thread defines the process as an executing entity, while the task defines the resources and environment in which the thread (or threads) of the process execute. A task is therefore the unit to which protections apply. One or more Mach threads executing within a task constitute what, at a higher level, is managed as a UNIX process.

The following table affords one perspective on the relationship between processes, threads, and tasks:

Process	**Task**	**Thread**
Address space	Address space	——
Stack	——	Stack
Program counter	——	Program counter

Having said all this, we will allow ourselves in future sections to shift between the terms "task" and "process", depending on what seems most natural in the different contexts.

Whereas processes (and their tasks) are highly protected from each other, the several threads of a single process are not. For example, a process cannot send a message to another process without explicit permission to do so, nor can it write into the memory of another process. But threads inherit all the communication channels, as well as the memory, of the parent process, and therefore they can easily cooperate or interfere with each other. Programming with threads requires considerable care.

A thread, as an executable entity requiring exactly one CPU, is the **unit of scheduling**. Where traditional UNIX systems schedule processes for execution, Mach (and OSF/1) schedule threads. A process can, as we have seen, produce several threads, each possessing its own, separate scheduling requirements.

It is important to recognize that **Mach threads are not POSIX threads**. The threads with which programmers usually have to do are implemented in OSF/1 using Mach threads, but the programmer interface is a higher-level one, conforming to the POSIX standard for threads (§11.1).

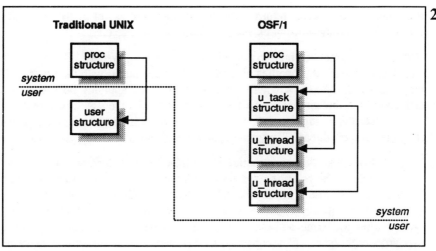

2.3

OSF/1 process data structures differ from traditional UNIX

UNIX processes execute in both "user mode" and "system mode". If you write an application to read two numbers typed at a terminal, add them together, and then write them to the terminal, the executing program begins carrying out your instructions in **user mode**. This means that the memory the instructions make use of, and the other resources they draw upon, are only those to which you as an individual user have right of access.

When, however, your program invokes a system call to read or write the terminal, a switch is made into **system mode**. In this mode it is operating system code—not your program in any direct sense—that is executing, although the operating system is acting on behalf of your program. In system mode, resources to which you do not have access are manipulated. For example, the terminal device driver handles I/O between system data structures and your terminal. Once the system call finishes, your program returns to user mode and continues execution. In other words, a system call is a request for operating system services, and those services are carried out in a highly privileged mode.

Traditional UNIX employs two key data structures to manage an executing process. The *proc* **structure** is used by the operating system to manage a process at the highest level: its scheduling, identification, swapping, and interruption. The *user* **structure** is maintained as part of user address space (that is, the restricted address space accessible when the process is running in user mode). It contains all the information that is needed only when the process is actually resident in memory—not swapped out (§4.1). This includes information about open files and other communication channels, size and location of the various memory segments of the process, return value (including error value) of the last system call, signal handling procedures, user identification, and so on.

How do these structures map to a Mach-based operating system? The *proc* structure largely describes properties of the Mach task associated with the process. On the other hand, the *user* structure contains information applying both to the task and also to the threads within the task. Thus, in OSF/1 the *user* structure is split in two: there is a single *u_task* structure, and in addition there is one *u_thread* structure for each thread. This change, however, is not visible to applications.

We said above that the *user* structure is contained in user memory on traditional UNIX systems. The operating system knows where to find this structure for any given process because it is placed at a known offset within the user address space of the process. However, this does not work when you have multiple threads, each sharing the same address space; the separate *u_thread* structures would overwrite each other. Consequently, OSF/1 carries both structures in system address space.

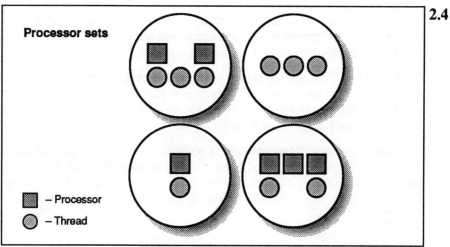

Processor sets

■ – Processor

● – Thread

2.4

OSF/1 allows you to match threads with processors

Threads, not processes, are the entities that get scheduled for execution. On multiprocessor systems, there are ways to control the allocation of threads to processors.

Processors can be organized into groups, or "clusters", called **processor sets**. Each set holds zero or more processors, and each processor is in one and only one set.

Likewise, every task is assigned to a processor set, and may run only on processors in that set. A task normally inherits the processor set of its parent. Similarly, each thread is assigned to the processor set of its task upon creation. Privileged system calls enable a task or thread to change its processor set. (If you want to make sure that the threads of an application do not compete with each other for execution time, you can assign them to separate processor sets.) Threads assigned to a null processor set are suspended.

The **default processor set** contains all processors and threads of the system.

A user-level server program—which can be modified or replaced by system administrators without reconfiguring the operating system—determines the allocation of processors to sets, the possible assignments of threads to processors, the number of processors a single application may tie up, and other matters of scheduling policy. By modifying this server program, it is possible define additional scheduling policies.

There are two scheduling policies currently supported. These apply to processor sets; that is, all the threads running on a processor set are subject to the scheduling policy established for that set. The policies are:

Fixed priority. This enables particular threads running on the processor set to receive preferential treatment. The priority is an integer representing the "importance" of the thread. More important threads are given execution time on a more urgent basis than less important threads.

Time-sharing policy. The goal here is equitable sharing of processors among threads. Each time-shared thread has not only a fixed priority, but also an additional, variable priority—depending on such things as its recent processor usage—that effectively lowers the priority in relation to fixed-priority threads.

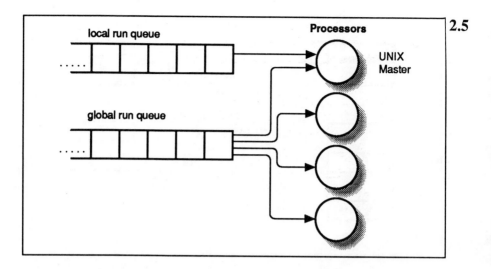

Dispatching threads for execution

A run queue is a set of threads awaiting execution. Such queues are of two types: a **global run queue** (one per processor set) for threads not requiring a particular processor; and a **local run queue** for threads waiting on a particular processor. Threads trying to execute unparallelized UNIX system calls and threads engaged in device I/O on unsymmetric hardware are examples of threads assigned to the local queue. Currently there is only one local run queue, for the processor known as the UNIX master. This is used solely for the support of those few parts of the operating system that have not been parallelized.

When a processor needs work, it first checks its local run queue (if any), then checks the global run queue, and finally, if it finds no work to do, runs a special **kernel idle thread**.

An important case is the dispatching of a runnable thread when there are idle processors. To speed this dispatch, the system maintains a list of idle processors. If this list is not empty when a thread is made runnable, then the thread is quickly dispatched to the first processor on the list.

On some architectures, however, it is advantageous for a newly runnable thread to resume execution on the same processor it last ran on. A feature that is conditionally compiled into OSF/1 causes a thread to be assigned to its last-used processor, if that processor is available.

When a thread is terminated, the operating system may elect to keep it "hanging around" in a pool of threads available for immediate allocation in response to new thread-creation requests. This use of **cache threads** can significantly reduce the overhead of thread creation.

2.6

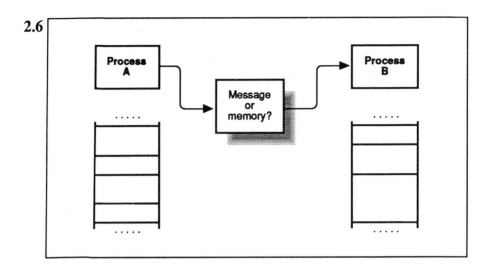

Messages and memory are closely related in OSF/1

Mach is sometimes referred to as "message-based". Most of its services can be triggered by sending messages (§3.1) to the operating system. At the same time, the designers of Mach realized that communication and memory handling are closely related, so that the two functions can stand in for each other. This is exemplified as well in OSF/1.

For example, a message can transfer a complete address space from one process to another, simply by mapping that address space into the message. This causes the same address space to be mapped into the receiving process. However, since copy-on-write (§4.2) techniques are employed, such a message does not result in any immediate data copying; pages of memory are actually copied into the address space of the receiving process only when an attempt to write those pages necessitates the transfer. If both processes are using the memory in a read-only manner, no copying will ever be necessary.

But if the message mechanisms can serve the purpose of memory transfer, so also can the machinery of memory management be used for sending what amounts to a message. That is, if one process uses a memory management system call to make a block of its memory available to another process (again using copy-on-write techniques), this easily becomes, in effect, the transfer of a message.

The general rule is that threads within the same process can communicate most efficiently using shared memory. Between processes, messages are perhaps the most natural way to communicate. However, threads within a process can send messages to each other, and different processes can share memory. If two processes are related as ancestor/dependent, they can share specified regions as readable, or both readable and writable. If the two processes are not related, they can share memory as readable—but attempts to write will result in separate copies being created, so that the memory is no longer shared. Two unrelated processes can share read/write memory by mapping the same file into their address spaces (§4.3).

In the next two chapters we will discuss, successively, Mach messages and memory management.

3

OSF/1 ARCHITECTURE:

Messages and Ports

IN THIS CHAPTER

- Interprocess communication via messages and ports
- Where ports come from, and how port rights are established
- The operating system manages ports and messages
- Threads can block on message queues
- Messages and distributed computing

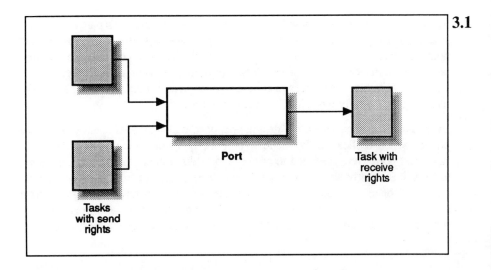

3.1

Port

Task with
receive
rights

Tasks
with send
rights

Interprocess communication via messages and ports

Threads can communicate by exchanging **messages**. This works between any two threads, whether or not they are in the same task. However, the main use for messages is between the threads of different tasks—messages are a means of **interprocess communication**. Threads within a single task can communicate more efficiently using shared memory. Messages are implemented in the Mach core of OSF/1.

Threads always send messages to **ports**, which are complete, unidirectional communication channels. Compare a BSD socket: a socket is an endpoint for communication, not a complete channel. Any task can usually find out the address of at least some sockets and send messages to them. Knowing the address of a socket does not tell you anything about the channels through which information may be flowing to or from that socket. A port, on the other hand, always denotes a link between one or more senders and a receiver. The operating system maintains data structures from which it can be known, at any given time, who has read and write permissions on a particular port.

What makes a port effectively a **unidirectional channel** is the fact that only one task may have receive rights on a port—although which task has the rights may change, and all the threads in a task share the receive rights. On the other hand, any number of tasks may have send rights. Thus, in a client-server application, a port can provide the server with a means to receive requests from multiple clients. (One thing the client can then do is to identify its own receive port so that the server can talk to it. But we'll get to that.) A task with receive rights on a port may also have send rights on the same port, so that it can send messages to itself.

Messages can be self-contained, with the message "enclosed" as part of the message data structure itself. Or else, with longer messages, the data structure can point to separate contents. As is common in OSF/1, these contents are manipulated by means of copy-on-write techniques that prevent memory replication whenever possible. The message contents get copied into the address space of the receiving thread only when and if it proves necessary.

Every message must specify a destination port, and may also specify a receive port to which replies can be made. The underlying operations supporting messages and ports were designed to accommodate distributed computing: in theory, at least, it is not known whether any given message arrives from a thread running on a local or remote machine—although certain differences of timing and error handling can be detected between the local and remote cases. Network message servers (§3.6) are implemented as Mach tasks communicating via messages.

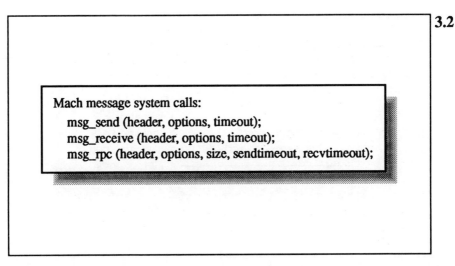

3.2

Mach message system calls:

msg_send (header, options, timeout);
msg_receive (header, options, timeout);
msg_rpc (header, options, size, sendtimeout, recvtimeout);

Synchronous and asynchronous aspects of messages

In each system call the *header* is the address of the message buffer that will contain the message (and its reply in the case of **msg_rpc**). This buffer might or might not contain the actual contents of the message. *options* provide various forms of control over the communication such as whether to return immediately if a software interrupt is received during message transmittal. The timeouts cause the request to be canceled if it can't be carried out within the designated time.

A thread issues a **msg_send** call to send a message. To receive a message, it calls **msg_receive**. To send a message and wait for the reply, it calls **msg_rpc**, where *size* is the maximum size allowed for the message reply. All three calls are synchronous with respect to the calling thread. For example, if a thread asks to receive a message on a particular port, and if there are no messages queued for that port, the thread will block until a message arrives. From the perspective of the process as a whole, however—with its ability to generate threads to wait on particular messages—the mechanism comes closer to being asynchronous in nature: the process, via its non-blocked threads, is free to continue its activity despite the fact that a particular thread may be waiting for a message.

Messages sent to a particular port enter a **message queue**, and are delivered to the receiving thread in the order of their receipt. However, the message-passing mechanisms support the idea of a **port set**, whereby a task with receive rights on several ports can combine them, in effect merging the separate queues into a single queue—rather like the UNIX *select* and *poll* system calls. This can be useful for I/O multiplexing.

3.3

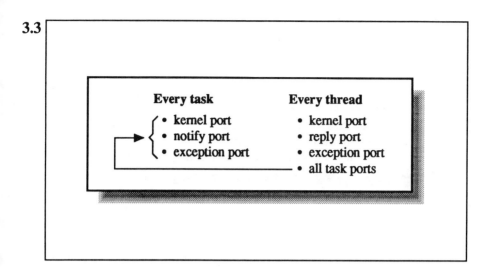

Where ports come from, and how port rights are established

Mach tasks are the basic units to which port privileges and protections apply. And since there is a one-to-one correlation between tasks and processes, (§2.2), these privileges may also be viewed as occurring on a per-process basis. All the threads within a task share the task's ports and port privileges—including those associated with other threads.

Every task has certain ports associated with it, established at time of task creation:

Task kernel port. This acts, in effect, as the name of the task. To execute a Mach system call affecting the task—say, a request to kill it—requires sending an appropriate message to the task's kernel port, which in turn requires send rights on the port. The kernel port is the "name" by which the operating system itself knows the task. The operating system has receive rights on this port.

Notify port. A task has receive rights on its own notify port. The operating system sends messages to this port whenever it needs to notify the task of certain events, such as the destruction of a port or a change in access privileges.

Exception port. A task has send rights on its own exception port. This can be used to implement an exception mechanism. For example, the default exception handler uses this port in conjunction with both the UNIX *signal(2)* mechanism and core dumps. The task exception port can also be useful to debuggers and performance analysis tools. OSF/1 offers programmers extensive control over the actions taken in response to certain exceptions, such as divide-by-zero.

The threads of a task automatically have the same rights on these ports that the task as a whole has. In addition, each individual thread has certain ports established for it at time of thread creation. These are—

Kernel thread port. As with the task kernel port, this is effectively the name by which the kernel knows the thread. The task as a whole is given send rights to this port. For example, in order to terminate thread A, any thread of the task would pass the kernel thread port name for thread A to the thread-termination system call.

Thread reply port. This port is used for receiving initialization messages from the parent task and responses from remote procedure calls issued with *msg_rpc* (§3.2).

Thread exception port. When a thread is created, its exception port is not activated. So long as this remains the case, exception messages applying to the thread are sent to the task exception port. If the thread subsequently activates its own exception port, then messages will be sent there.

Note again that port privileges apply to tasks in their entirety. Thus, not only do these thread ports become available to the whole task—that is, to all the other threads in the task—but, also, each thread shares the rights described above for the ports associated with the whole task at task-creation.

In addition, a task may gain rights to ports in other, unrelated tasks—and may also pass off its own rights—all subject to appropriate permissions. Furthermore, besides **send** and **receive** rights on ports, there are also **grant** rights: the rights to "give away" send and receive rights on particular ports. Grant rights may be passed to other tasks.

Finally, a task can revoke a child task's rights on the parent's ports.

Since ports are complete communication channels, with sending and receiving privileges managed by the operating system, the question arises: how does a user application gain access to a channel that it did not inherit?

Suppose, for example, that the application wants to inquire of a print server about the status of a print queue. To begin with, the application must know some conventional name for the server, as maintained in system databases or given in the documentation. Using that name, a thread of the application requests port rights to the print server from the system's name server—which previously will have been given grant rights from the print server. The name server returns the actual port rights to the application, using the return port supplied in the application's original request.

This leaves still unanswered the question: how can the application send its initial request to the name server. The answer is that, since created tasks inherit send rights to their ancestor tasks, and since the name server is the ancestor of all other tasks, every task can send messages to the name server.

From an application's standpoint, a port is simply an integer. The operating system maintains a mapping from the port designators of individual threads to the actual port data structures. The same designator in different threads may refer to different ports.

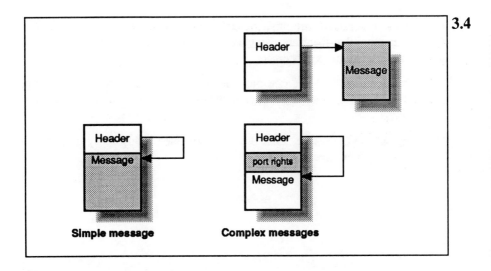

3.4

Simple message   Complex messages

The operating system manages ports and messages

There are two kinds of messages:

In **simple messages** the content of the message is included right along with the message data structure. Another requirement for simple messages is that they contain no port rights. If the content of a message is a request relating to port rights, then it will not be classified as simple.

Every message failing to qualify as a simple message is classified as **complex**. Complex messages require the operating system to carry out additional functions:

- verify that the message body to which the message data structure points is "real"

- make sure that any request for port rights, or granting of port rights, is consistent with existing permissions

Not only does the operating system verify certain message information; it may actually effect appropriate translations. For example, if a thread sends an inquiry to a local print server in a networked environment, and if that server does not currently exist, the operating system may translate the message addressee so as to re-route the message to a print server on a remote machine.

While message-sending through ports offers different processes a method for communicating "directly" with each other, this communication is mediated by the operating system. The ports themselves are operating system data structures, and the queues in which messages are placed are in system address space.

In fact, some system calls are implemented as messages. This is as good a place as any to mention that there are two classes of system calls within OSF/1, so far as their implementation is concerned:

* **Mach system calls** are carried out simply as messages passed to the calling tasks' kernel port. Such a message includes the system call name and arguments.

* Traditional **UNIX system calls** are software traps followed by a switch to privileged system execution.

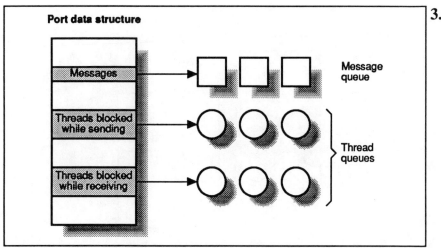

Port data structure   **3.5**

Messages → Message queue

Threads blocked while sending

Threads blocked while receiving

Thread queues

Threads can block on message queues

Like most any queue, the queues associated with Mach ports can become full. That may happen because messages are being sent to the port at a very high rate, or because no process is bothering to read the port. If a thread tries to write to such a port, the thread **blocks**—its execution is suspended. The operating system re-awakens the thread if and when a message is removed from the queue—or after some specified period of time (timeout).

Similarly, if a thread requests to receive a message from a port for which no messages are enqueued, it will block. The operating system re-awakens the thread when a message arrives—or after a timeout.

The kernel maintains a data structure for each port in the system. That structure, among other things, points to:

* the list of enqueued messages

* a list of threads that have blocked upon trying to read an empty queue

* a list of threads that have blocked while trying to write to a full queue

A port becomes defunct when the process possessing receive rights to it dies or otherwise allows its rights to disappear without passing them on to another process. The operating system notifies each process possessing send rights on the port that the port has been deleted. Similarly, it awakens all threads blocked while trying to send messages to the port, and causes the *msg_send* calls of these threads to return with an error.

3.6

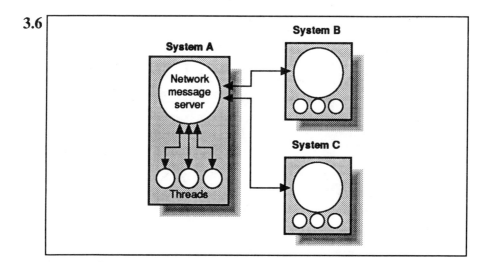

Messages and distributed computing

So far we have spoken primarily of communication between processes on the same machine. However, Mach was written with distributed computing in mind—and, in fact, OSF/1 extends the message/port mechanism so that it applies to processes on Mach-based hosts anywhere in a network. The key element here is the **network message server**.

One copy of this server runs on each system in the network. A network message server functions as a message exchange, accepting messages from local ports and forwarding them, when necessary, to servers on remote ports. Servers also pass messages between themselves regarding the status of operations in progress and the location of services distributed throughout the network.

A given network message server therefore plays the additional role of a simple port name service. Ports throughout the network can register with the network message server, and in turn the server provides a port look-up service for applications with inquiring minds.

Network message servers offer yet other services:

- **data type conversion** between processes running on separate machines with incompatible hardware

- enforcement of Mach IPC **network security** policies

4

OSF/1 ARCHITECTURE:

Virtual Memory

IN THIS CHAPTER

- Some basic concepts relating to virtual memory ...

- ... And a general principle

- Some features of OSF/1 virtual memory

- Managing processes with memory in mind

- Virtual memory and physical memory

- What is a virtual memory object?

- Address maps

- The larger picture

- Page faults and paging out

- Mapping virtual addresses to physical addresses

- External memory management

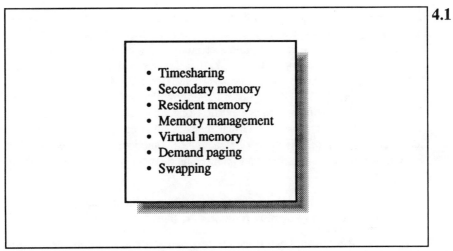

- Timesharing
- Secondary memory
- Resident memory
- Memory management
- Virtual memory
- Demand paging
- Swapping

4.1

Some basic concepts relating to virtual memory...

We spoke earlier of **timesharing** (§2.1), whereby—even on single-processor systems—multiple programs can *appear* to run at the same time. They gain this appearance by virtue of extremely rapid, alternate turns at execution. On the other hand, multiprocessor systems allow separate programs, processes, and threads to execute with true simultaneity, one thread of execution per processor.

If you write and compile an application, it normally is stored on disk—in what is often called **secondary memory**. When you execute the application, the system loads needed segments of it from disk into primary or **main memory**, where it is said to be **resident**. The CPU has direct access to the instructions and data of a resident program. On all timesharing and multiprocessing systems, more than one program may be resident at once. (It would be impossibly expensive to read a program from disk and then write it back out to disk each time it gained a moment of CPU execution time.)

Where do these various resident programs actually reside? Clearly, they cannot all reside at the same location in main memory, for they would then overwrite each other. It is part of the operating system's **memory management** function to place each program—actually, each process or task—at a place in main memory that does not conflict with other resources.

This, however, raises a difficulty: if a program does not know where it will sit in memory, how does it calculate its memory addresses? How, for example, does it know where in memory a particular variable can be found?

Part of the answer lies in the notion of **virtual memory**. Every program, as written and compiled, imagines itself to live in an ideal memory space. That is, the text and data of the program consume a certain amount of space, and the program has the luxury of assuming, without risk, that this space is addressable in a standard way—say, beginning with address zero and (for a 100K-sized program) continuing to address 100K. (This ignores the program's stack, which normally must be viewed as occupying a separate portion of memory.) This idealized address space is known as the program's virtual memory. It is up to other facilities—the linker, run-time loader, and memory management functions—to make everything "come out right" for a program that pictures its memory this way. To be extraordinarily simplistic:

- the compiler and linker make program addresses "relocatable"—relative to some as-yet-unknown starting position—so that ...

- ... the run-time loader can place the program at a known location (or distribute it among many locations) in memory, at which time it can also translate program addresses correctly; and ...

- ... the operating system can establish tables mapping the program's ideal, or virtual, addresses to actual physical addresses in main memory.

There are further complications. Not all of the text and data of a program needs to be resident in order for the program to be executing at any given time. Only the current instructions and the immediately required data must be accessible. By not necessarily trying to keep all of every executing program in main memory, the operating system can manage more running programs at once than might otherwise be the case. It thereby makes more efficient use of main memory.

But, of course, there is a cost in complexity for this advantage: the operating system must now provide mechanisms for **demand paging**. This is the means by which additional blocks ("pages") of a program are read into main memory on demand—when they are needed—and other pages are written back out to disk when main memory gets too full to accommodate the next pages it needs to read in. This two-way process is known more briefly as "paging".

When space in physical memory becomes especially short, it may become necessary to do more than casually move individual pages in and out. To make more room, the operating system may **swap out** an entire process (except for certain key data structures required in order to swap the process back in later and restore its execution state).

During all this paging and swapping, it is not necessary to write read-only pages to secondary memory, since they already reside there and do not undergo change in their passage through main memory. (This applies, for example, to the instruction, or "text", portion of a process.) As to writable pages—such as the stack and writable data—a special region of secondary memory, called the **swap file**, is reserved for the paging and swapping activity.

In summary, we have a picture of multiple processes, fragments of which are scattered throughout main and secondary memory, and each of which is executing in an idealized virtual memory environment that looks like a clean expanse of privately owned, uncontested space. All of which makes for the most arcane and esoteric indirection in an operating system's memory management.

Understandably desiring to simplify things wherever possible, the designers of OSF/1 employed the Mach virtual memory facilities, rather than build upon the approaches and data structures encumbering the early UNIX systems.

4.2

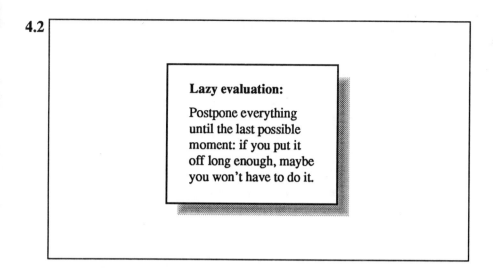

Lazy evaluation:

Postpone everything
until the last possible
moment: if you put it
off long enough, maybe
you won't have to do it.

...And a general principle

Lazy evaluation is a principle with high status in the OSF/1 virtual memory world. For it turns out that many things operating systems in the past have felt obligated to do—just aren't necessary. No one would notice if these things were delayed or, in some cases, left undone. So the designers of more recent operating systems have tried to step out from under the obligations. For OSF/1, this means, among other things, that

- no maps showing the relation of virtual memory to physical memory are created until a thread refers to the virtual memory in question (map-on-reference)

- no pages of physical memory are assigned to a process until the process actually needs to use them

- no page is copied until two copies are necessary—they can be shared by different processes so long as no conflicting use is made of them (copy-on-write)

- no pages in the swap file in secondary memory are allocated for a process until the process actually needs them

Here is one example of the benefits of lazy evaluation: if a program maps a file into its address space (§4.3), no part of the file actually gets "read in" to main memory until the program refers to it—and then only the required pages are read in. On its part, the program has access to the entire file as if it were fully mapped into its address space, while on the operating system's part, the mapping work is done only as needed. If the program ends up using only a few bits of data in a very large file, the rest of the file is never brought into main memory.

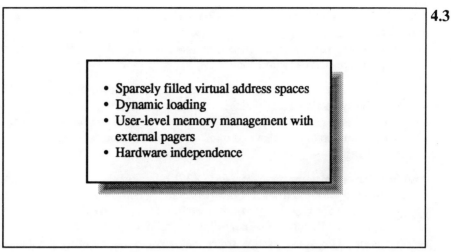

4.3

- Sparsely filled virtual address spaces
- Dynamic loading
- User-level memory management with external pagers
- Hardware independence

Some features of OSF/1 virtual memory

There are a few other general features of the virtual memory system worth mentioning before we take a look inside that system.

The virtual address space of a process is allowed to be **sparse**. This means that program virtual memory can contain islands of data with large tracts of "vacant space" between them. While the program has the luxury of continuing to treat this memory as a single, contiguous address space, the operating system avoids the overhead of actually mapping the unused portions of memory. Here are two examples showing why a programmer might want to take advantage of sparse address spaces:

- FORTRAN programs—which traditionally cannot allocate memory dynamically—often initialize huge arrays to receive data from some source. These arrays have to be made large enough to handle the maximum number of data points—and therefore may remain largely empty on program runs with few data points.

- Under OSF/1 a program can dynamically read files into its address space. It may well be that a program needs to append large amounts of data to such a file. The use of sparse address spaces allows the program to provide that space without its actually having to be managed in detail by the memory management system except so far as the additional data actually arrives.

The ability to map various objects, including files, into the address space of a process is one aspect of **dynamic loading** (§10.8), by which executing programs can load additional program modules "on the fly". Among other things, dynamic loading greatly speeds up program development for large applications. When an individual module in the program is changed and re-compiled, it can be read into the otherwise unchanged program at run time, without there being a need to re-compile and re-link the whole thing.

OSF/1 supports **user-level memory management**. This means that it is possible to change the system's paging policies without re-configuring the operating system itself. (This is part of the overall effort to remove as many functions as possible out of the operating system and into "user space".) One does this by writing an **external pager**.

Also in regard to memory management, OSF/1 allows both **paging to files** and **paging to a raw disk partition**. A raw partition is a portion of a disk outside all file systems. Paging to such a partition therefore saves the overhead of file system management. The choice of pages for paging out is determined by a **least-recently-used** strategy: in general, pages that have been inactive for the longest time are selected for paging out first.

The approach to virtual memory taken in the Mach-based OSF/1 operating system is intended to be as **hardware-independent** as possible, with the device-dependent code cleanly separated from the rest.

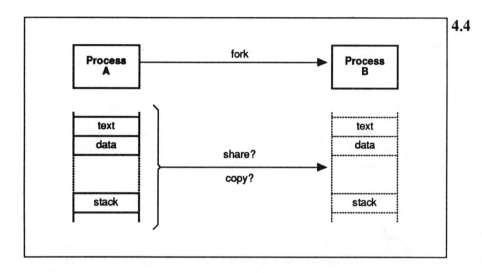

4.4

Managing processes with memory in mind

When a process forks, creating a child process, there are various possibilities regarding memory. The original UNIX fork was the duplication of an entire process; after the fork, there were now two processes—with two fully allocated and copied memory spaces, two identical sets of file descriptors, and nearly every other resource likewise replicated. The crucial difference between the two processes lay in their separate process IDs. Of course, it was common after a fork for one of the processes—typically the child—to overlay itself with a new program by means of an *exec* system call—requiring a second massive copying of memory. This overall mechanism provided a way for processes to carry out specific subsets of their activity with little programming overhead.

The operating system overhead in memory copying, however, was severe, and more recent versions of UNIX have attempted to provide less expensive alternatives. OSF/1 gives the programmer several options. One of these is the traditional sort of fork: the duplication of an entire process. Overall, there are these possibilities:

The child inherits copies of all regions of parental memory. This is the traditional policy, expensive in overhead, and often not necessary.

The child shares all regions of parental memory. In this case, both parent and child can modify the memory, and each will see the other's modifications. The creation of the new process in this case is quite inexpensive, since no massive areas of memory need to be copied. (The stack, however, must be copied. Every thread has its own stack. Remember that a simple process is implemented as a single Mach thread executing within the context of a single Mach task. It is a thread that must request the fork, and therefore it is the thread's stack that is copied to create the stack of the single thread embodying the newly created process.)

The child may inherit or share only portions of parental memory. The parent can specify specific regions of memory to be omitted from the child.

It is worth noting as well that a process can grant read, write, and execute permission for its memory regions to unrelated tasks. This memory sharing device becomes a means for **interprocess communication**.

Once a process has been created, there are a number of virtual memory system calls with which it can manage its own memory—in addition to the traditional UNIX calls:

vm_allocate. Add to the process's virtual memory space by allocating new, zero-filled memory. This memory will be page-aligned, and its size will be an integral multiple of the page size.

vm_deallocate. Remove a region of virtual memory from the process's address space.

vm_map. Map a region of currently-used memory into the process's address space. This could be a file on disk.

vm_inherit. Change the current inheritance value for regions of process memory. The inheritance value determines whether child processes will receive copies of the region, or will share the region.

vm_read. Read from a memory region belonging to another process, if the region's protection value permits it.

vm_write. Write to a memory region belonging to another process, if the region's protection value permits it.

vm_copy. Copy data from a memory region belonging to another process, if the region's protection value permits it.

vm_protect. Change the current protection value (read-write permissions) for regions of process memory.

vm_region. Inquire about memory regions belonging to other processes. For example, what are the current protection and inheritance values for these regions?

vm_statistics. Inquire about the operating system's virtual memory usage patterns.

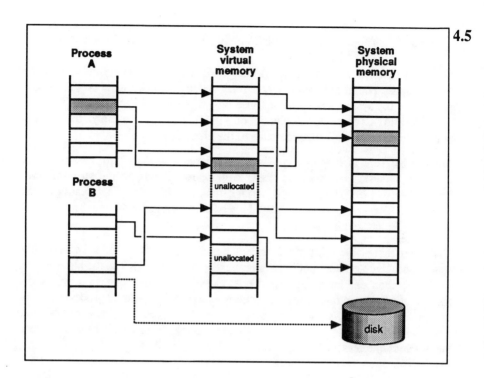

4.5

Virtual memory and physical memory

We have already given some indication of what we mean by virtual memory—but that was largely from the point of view of a process. We must also learn, when speaking of "virtual memory", to see with the operating system's eyes. This operating system is feverishly trying to coordinate the actual placement in main memory and secondary memory of many different processes, each of which is enjoying a view of itself as possessing the whole of an idealized memory. But the operating system does not do this directly; if processes can dream up a virtual, highly ordered and simplified landscape, then so can the operating system. In other words, the operating system itself views all the current processes, with their separate virtual memory spaces, against a larger virtual backdrop that contains all those spaces. This backdrop is again dealt with as a continuous span of virtual memory running from zero to some very high value. The difference is that the operating system also knows—in excruciating detail—how this larger virtual landscape maps to every acre of the local real estate.

So the operating system does two things we want to know about:

- it maps the virtual address space of processes to its own, more global perspective on virtual address space.

- it maps some portion of the global virtual address space to physical memory

Notice that, so far as each process is concerned, it contains an unhindered virtual address space potentially much larger than system physical memory. Yet at any given time the system may have mapped only a portion of each process's virtual memory into its own global picture of virtual memory—namely, the portion required by the current execution state of the process.

So long as there is indeed a consistent, accurate mapping from system virtual memory to physical memory, no matter how indirect it may be, the operating system is free to take advantage of "virtual thinking" in most of its dealings with processes. Two points where it must descend into physical mappings are in handling page faults—which we will discuss later—and in doing I/O.

One other thing. We pointed out earlier that OSF/1 does not allocate swap file space for a given process until space is actually required. This is one place where lazy evaluation can cause trouble. For it can happen that when, in a tight spot, the operating system finds itself needing to swap out a very large process, there is inadequate space left in the swap file to receive the process. The outcome of such a scenario—in release 1.0—may be a system crash. There are efforts to correct the problem in release 1.1.

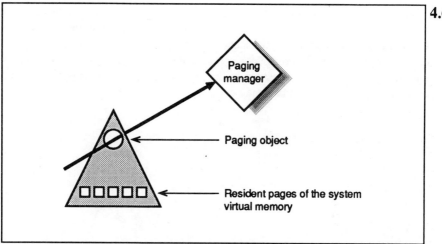

4.6

Paging manager

Paging object

Resident pages of the system virtual memory

What is a virtual memory object?

To start with, it is best to view the **virtual memory object** as nothing more than a data structure—and so it is. However, it is a slightly odd data structure: if you push on it at just the right places—it tends to *jump*. But first a little explanation.

Virtual memory objects are maintained by the operating system. Each object corresponds to a set of contiguous pages in system virtual memory—perhaps a group of pages that were allocated to some process at the same time. Thus, the "system virtual memory" shown in §4.5 can actually be thought of as an ordered sequence of memory objects. Each of these objects contains:

- a list of the **resident pages** in this object—that is, the pages currently present in physical memory

- a second kind of object—a paging object—corresponding to the pages in this object that are not resident, but are either paged out or not yet paged in for the first time

Again, just think of this **paging object** as another data structure. In this case the data structure happens to contain a pointer to the **paging manager** associated with these pages. (This will be either the default paging manager of the operating system, or a user-created one.) Actually, the "pointer" is the name of the port (§3.1) at which the paging manager is listening. So we can view the paging object as a port through which non-resident pages of the virtual memory object can be pulled into main memory.

That is the peculiar thing about an object: though it is permissible to think of it as a data structure, certain parts of the data structure are "hot buttons" for specific operating system activities; you access that part of the data structure in certain defined ways in order to *do something*. In this case, the right sort of poke on the paging object results in a message to the paging manager that says, "we need to bring in a page from secondary memory".

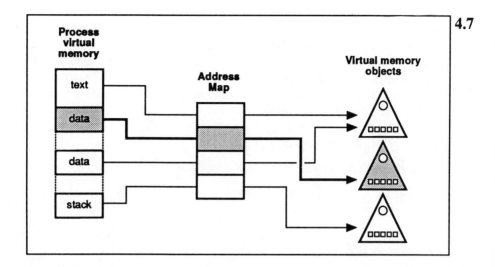

Address maps

The mapping from process to system virtual memory shown in section 4.6—if it is to be manageable—needs to be broken down into smaller pieces. Both virtual and physical memory in modern computers tend to be very large—perhaps billions of bytes—and any single data structure trying to characterize every page of this memory must unavoidably be massive. Processes, on the other hand, tend to require chunks of memory in relatively small blocks.

Virtual memory objects, in conjunction with **address maps,** offer a means to manage numerous, separate regions of memory more efficiently.

The illustration shows the virtual address space of an executing process. (Remember that, from the process's own point of view, this is conveniently viewed as extending from some low address—say zero—continuously through as high an address as is needed to hold the entire text and data segments of the process.) The dotted lines show the parts of this idealized address space that, for the moment at least, do not contain text or data. That is, each page of virtual address space between solid lines corresponds to a page of physical memory, whether resident or swapped out. The virtual memory space between dotted lines does not as yet correspond to any physical memory.

The operating system maintains an address map for each process. This maps each successive segment of the process's virtual memory to a memory object. Each segment has certain characteristics—including read/write permissions—in common; if the process changes the permissions on a page in the middle of a segment, then new address map entries are created to represent the two or three resulting subsegments.

Older UNIX systems maintain "page tables" reflecting the entire virtual address space of a process. These are usually data structures used by hardware for translating virtual addresses to physical addresses. This can become quite expensive, if the process consumes many megabytes of memory. In OSF/1 the address map contains entries only for those memory segments that are actually allocated and correspond to physical pages in main or secondary memory. Consequently, sparsely filled address spaces can be managed quite efficiently: they don't require huge address maps.

There are three things to note here (despite appearances in the illustrations):

* an address map entry may map a memory segment to *some portion* of the pages represented by a memory object, rather than to all the pages

* different memory segments of a given process may map to the same or different memory objects

* memory segments of different processes may map to the same memory object—such as when two processes share the same text (instruction) segment. Memory segments of different processes may also map to the same object, but to different memory blocks within that object.

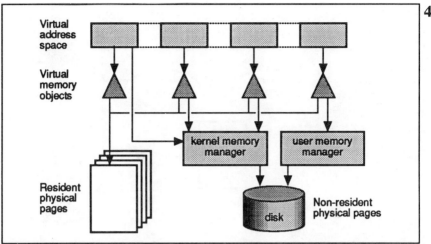

4.8

The larger picture

A process's address space can be represented as a list of address ranges, or segments, each of which has certain common characteristics, and each of which maps to some subset of pages in a particular virtual memory object. This object corresponds to a portion of the global virtual memory managed by the operating system, which in turn maps to resident and non-resident physical memory.

What happens when a process maps a new chunk of memory into its address space? It depends on where the memory is added, but a typical case looks like this: an existing data segment of the process is extended by inclusion of contiguous virtual memory. If

* the new memory has the same permissions and other relevant characteristics as the segment to which it is being joined; and

* the memory object for that segment already contains the newly allocated system virtual memory,

then the addition may be reflected merely in an extended page range being written into a pre-existing address map entry. Otherwise, a new map entry may have to be created, pointing to the same or a different memory object.

The illustration above is rather simplistic, for it shows each memory segment of the process mapping to a single memory object, and omits the address map altogether. Also, nothing is shown of the details of virtual-to-physical address mapping.

4.9

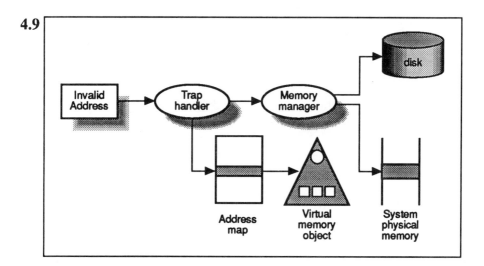

Page faults and paging out

So far we have restricted ourselves to discussion of process and system virtual memory, acknowledging that some pages of this memory may be resident, and some non-resident. What happens when the process tries to read or write a location on a non-resident page? Several things:

1. First, since the page is in fact non-resident, the operating system possesses no valid mapping from the virtual memory address of the location in question to an actual resident physical address. (We haven't discussed such mappings at all so far, but they do exist.) Consequently, an invalid address ends up being used, which trips a **hardware-dependent trap**.

2. The trap handler in turn invokes the operating system's **page fault handler**, passing it relevant information such as the failed address (in the virtual address space of the *process*) and the associated address map.

3. The page fault handler is now able to peruse the suspicious address map entry, from which it can determine the virtual memory object—and the particular page within virtual memory—for which the fault occurred.

4. Having identified the required page of virtual memory, the page fault handler passes a request to a **paging manager** (the default system manager or an external—user-created—manager) to bring the page into resident memory. Resident page tables (§4.10) showing the physical address of every page of system virtual memory make this possible.

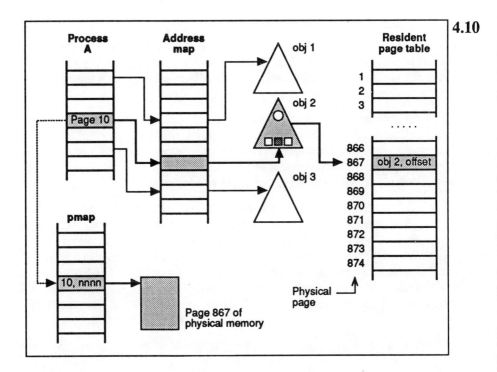

Mapping virtual addresses to physical addresses

We have yet to speak about physical addressing. There is associated with every process a physical map, or **pmap.** This map normally contains entries for some or all of the pages in the virtual address space of the process, specifying a physical address of each page. The pmap is the key hardware-dependent structure of the memory management system.

A closely related structure—the **resident page table,** is hardware-independent, but in conjunction with hardware-related data it enables memory management routines to reconstruct pmaps from scratch. How can this table be hardware-independent, and yet be used to construct tables of physical addresses? The resident page table is simply an array of entries, one for each page of physical memory; but it does not contain actual physical addresses. Nevertheless, because the hardware-dependent routines can convert "68th page of physical memory" to "physical address *nnnn*", the table is all that is required for mapping system virtual memory to physical memory.

The illustration, then, shows a sequence of pages in process virtual memory, one of which—page 10—is shaded in the drawing. The pmap entry for this page—if it exists—happens to show that page 10 has a particular physical address—the address of the 867th page of physical memory. At the same time, This same page 10 is mapped into a virtual memory object as the second of three pages in the object. The resident page table, in turn, shows that this page of system virtual memory—which is located in *obj2* with an offset of 1 page, corresponds to the 867th page of physical memory.

In this scheme, a pmap acts as a cache of physical page addresses for a single process. It does not keep track of non-resident pages, which are managed by the virtual memory object mechanisms. Furthermore, some or all of a pmap may be removed by the memory management functions, in which case the pmap will be re-built as necessary directly from the resident page table.

It is clear that the pmap, resident page table, and virtual memory objects divide up the data structure that, in most earlier UNIX systems, was embodied in the page table. The latter mapped virtual addresses to physical addresses for the whole of system memory, and the pages of all processes were managed by means of this table. By contrast, OSF/1 isolates the fully machine-dependent structure in a small, per-process table (pmap) that acts like a cache. And it employs "detached" memory objects for much of the management of virtual memory operations. The OSF/1 developers saw certain advantages in their approach:

- due to a richer set of data structures, certain things are easier to access and manage

- hiding machine dependencies in one place tends to simplify things

- this whole approach makes it possible to avoid the considerable overhead of setting up the entire address space of a process when it first starts running

4.11

External pagers
- User-written
- Applications not portable
- Efficiency gain for special purposes

External memory management

We have referred a number of times in passing to external, or user-written, pagers. "User-written" here (as often throughout this book) is not to be taken casually as referring to any programmer on a system. The point of the term is that the operating system explicitly provides interfaces to allow for paging managers that execute in "user space" and therefore do not require reconfiguration of the operating system itself.

Vendors porting OSF/1 to specific platforms, and end users developing highly sophisticated applications, are the ones most likely to take advantage of this interface. However, since external paging managers are not governed by any standards, those programs making use of such managers may be quite non-portable.

Nevertheless, the ability to create and use external pagers could prove valuable. For example, a network file server might provide access to files on different machines. A client would request a remote file from the server (paging manager), which would create a virtual memory object representing the file. The paging object in this memory object would be the port at which the file server listens. Then, when the client caused a page fault by trying to access the remote file, the operating system would automatically notify the server. In addition to negotiating (possibly with a second server) on a remote system and obtaining the actual data pages comprising the file, the local server would be responsible for providing the operating system with any information it requires when handling page faults.

A paging manager directly manages page-in and page-out (§4.9). In addition, it can use a message interface to the operating system to manage physical page mapping indirectly. If a paging manager is lax in carrying out some of its responsibilities, the operating system steps forward in a backup role.

5

OSF/1 ARCHITECTURE:

Dynamic Device Configuration

IN THIS CHAPTER

- Device drivers
- Device tables
- Hard-wired interrupt handlers
- Dynamically-configured interrupt tables

5.1

> **Devices** are accessed as special files in */dev*
> - Block devices use buffering
> - Character (raw) devices do not buffer
>
> Examples of devices:
> - Terminals
> - Disks
> - Tapes
>
> A device driver controls the operation of a device.

Device drivers

A **device driver** is a part of the kernel used to control operation of a peripheral device, such as a terminal, disk drive, tape drive, or printer. Device drivers are machine-dependent, so OSF only supplies device drivers for the reference ports used in development of OSF/1. Vendors porting OSF/1 to various platforms normally supply their own device drivers.

A given device may be treated as either a **block** device or a **character** (or **raw**) device, accessed via a special file in the */dev* directory.

- **block devices** are treated as random access storage devices that are designed to transfer data a block at a time, where a block is commonly 512 or 1024 bytes. Buffering mechanisms are used to regulate data flow between a block device and the kernel. Examples of block devices include disk drives or tape drives.

- **character** (or **raw**) devices do not use any buffering. Examples of character devices include terminals and modems.

Device files are distinguished from other files by either the "block" or "character special" file type stored in their inodes. Character devices use a character interface, and disk and tape devices are generally given both a block and character interface.

5.2

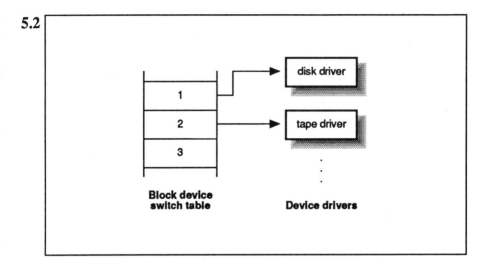

Device tables

In configuring a device special file on a UNIX system, an administrator uses the *mknod* command, as follows:

```
# mknod /dev/ttyi1n c 2 14
```

The first argument to *mknod* is the pathname of the special device file, and the second argument is the file type (in this case "c" for "character").

The third argument is the **major device number**, indicating the device type and which driver to use. Since this is a character device, the major device number must correspond to an entry in the character device switch tables. Multiple devices can have the same device driver, so the **minor device number**, which is the fourth argument, is used to distinguish them. In the example, *ttyi1n* is the 14th terminal to be configured using the terminal driver, so it gets a minor device number of 14.

Each entry in the character or block device switch tables (**cdevsw** or **bdevsw**) is a structure containing entry points for the associated driver. A problem on some UNIX systems is that if the device tables are not properly configured, the system may crash since a driver might produce a fault when attempting to access an absent controller.

Like BSD systems, OSF/1 **automatically configures device drivers** at boot time and statically links them into the kernel. Devices are automatically "activated" only if they are present at boot time.

The *probe*( ) and *attach*( ) routines are the entry points to the device driver that are used at boot time for autoconfiguration. The *probe*( ) routine is called to determine whether the device is present, and the *attach*( ) routine initializes (attaches) the device if the *probe*( ) routine has determined that it is available.

On systems that are not autoconfigured, the device table has to be manually edited by the system administrator if a controller is removed, to prevent a crash at boot time.

5.3

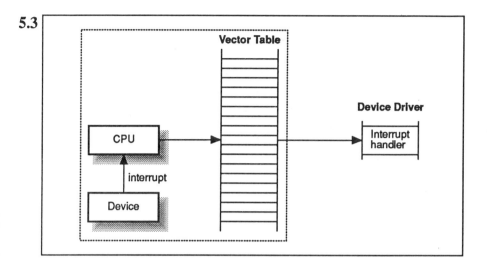

Hard-wired interrupt handlers

In earlier UNIX operating systems, interrupt-handling is "hardwired". Since device drivers must be capable of responding to interrupts, this means that device drivers, too, are hardwired into the operating system when the system is configured, or at system boot time. Here is a generic picture of how interrupts work:

When a device needs attention, it signals this fact by sending an **interrupt** to the CPU. An interrupt is a hardware mechanism, and what happens in response to it is hardware-dependent, but typically certain identifying information sent along with the interrupt provides a means for the CPU to select an entry in a **vector table**. The content of this entry is the address of a signal-handling routine appropriate for this particular device.

If, for example, it is a terminal that sent the interrupt, then the identifying information sent along with the interrupt effectively selects the vector table entry containing the address of the terminal device driver's interrupt-handling routine. After saving certain state information—such as the next instruction that was going to be executed when the interrupt was received—the system jumps to the address of the interrupt-handling routine. This routine processes the interrupt—say, by reading or writing to the device. When the device driver routine finishes, the system picks up where it left off before the interrupt by returning to the saved instruction.

If a device driver should somehow be removed from the system during operation (which is, of course, impossible), the receipt of an interrupt whose corresponding vector table entry pointed at that driver's (now missing) interrupt-handling routine would cause unpredictable behavior and a likely crash. The addition of a device driver during system operation would be ineffective, since there would be no way to re-adjust the interrupt mechanisms so as to call up the driver's interrupt handler.

5.4

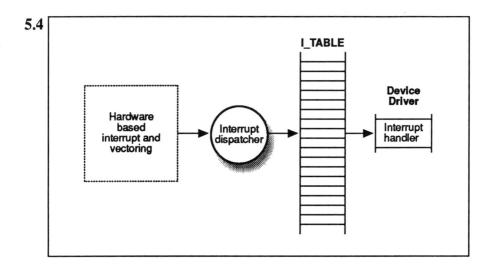

Dynamically-configured interrupt tables

OSF/1 provides **dynamic configuration of device drivers** while the system is running, with the aid of the run-time loader (§10.8). This is only one example of a module that can be dynamically loaded into the kernel. Other modules that can be loaded or unloaded from a running system are **file systems, streams modules and drivers**, and **network protocols**.

In order to dynamically configure device drivers, OSF/1 has devised a method for adding or removing interrupt handlers at run time. Instead of sending an interrupt directly from the vector table to the associated interrupt handler, as shown previously, the interrupt is detoured to an **interrupt dispatcher**, as shown above. The interrupt dispatcher consults an interrupt table (I_TABLE) for the appropriate handler, and then forwards the interrupt to the handler. The interrupt table is initialized at autoconfiguration time by the interrupt dispatcher, but the dispatcher also provides routines for adding, deleting, enabling and disabling handlers dynamically.

Due to the hardware-dependent nature of interrupts, OSF/1 supplies interrupt dispatcher code only for its reference ports.

The run-time loader loads the new driver into the rest of the operating system. The *configure()* routine, an entry point into the device driver, is then called to link it with the rest of the kernel. The *configure()* routine is necessary only if the *probe()* and *attach()* routines have not been called at boot time.

The *configure*( ) routine has two discrete functions:

- It links its device interrupt handler into the rest of the kernel using the interrupt dispatcher. This is accomplished through a pair of routines: *handler_add*( ), which registers a new interrupt handler, and *handler_enable*( ), which "turns on" a registered interrupt handler.

- It creates entries in the character device switch table (**cdevsw**) or the block device switch table (**bdevsw**)—or both—using the routines *cdevsw_add*( ) and *bdevsw_add*( ). These entries are the means by which the appropriate driver routines are invoked in response to system calls.

In both cases, the administrator either supplies a major device number or is assigned one. This device number can be used with *mknod* to assign device files to the new device driver (§5.2).

6

OSF/1 ARCHITECTURE:

File Systems

IN THIS CHAPTER

- Virtual file system: raising the level of abstraction
- Vnodes represent files independently of file systems
- Mounting a file system
- The operating system buffers file I/O
- The structure of the S5 file system
- Inodes map the successive blocks of a file to physical blocks on disk
- The structure of UFS
- Some features of UFS under OSF/1
- The NFS file system
- Some features of NFS
- How to keep NFS client caches relatively consistent
- NFS servers perform automatic write-through

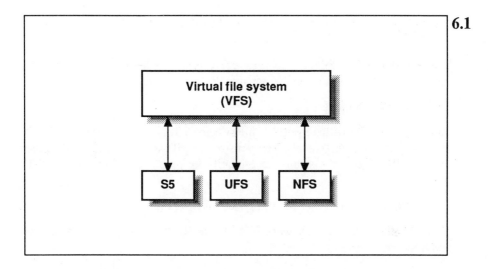

Virtual file system: raising the level of abstraction

Traditional UNIX file systems embody an **abstraction**: a set of uniform "file" data structures in the operating system is used to represent individual files on disk, the disk itself, pipes, sockets, and other physical devices capable of I/O. This has a great advantage—namely, it allows a program to use the same I/O system calls without knowing what sort of communication channel it is connected to. Such a program can therefore be used in a shell pipeline, and its output can be redirected to a file or to a terminal—all without changing the program itself.

Note that "file system" was therefore an ambiguous term. It could refer, in the narrow sense, to the collection of text and data files on disk, such as the file you call up with an editor; or, it could embrace the entire, unified set of mechanisms for accessing files in the broader, more abstract sense.

At first, UNIX systems supported only one file system abstraction. Today, however, there are different types of file systems running on UNIX systems. To make those systems compatible with each other, it is necessary to deal with entire file systems abstractly, much as UNIX has always dealt with the notion of an individual file abstractly. A **virtual file system** accomplishes exactly that.

A virtual file system provides a common way to refer to files regardless of the file systems in which they reside. The operating system modules implementing the virtual file system translate generic, file-related requests into the terms required by the actual file systems.

OSF/1's virtual file system derives from Berkeley UNIX and is very similar to Sun's VFS.

Requests relating to sockets and networking protocols do not pass through the virtual file system, but are handled separately.

OSF/1 currently supports:

S5 file system. This is the System V file system (6.5). The code implementing S5 is not parallelized. In general, operations on this file system will be slower than the UFS file system. S5 is supplied primarily for purposes of UNIX compatibility.

UFS. Parallelized. The "native" file system of OSF/1 (§6.7).

NFS. Parallelized. Sun's Network File System (§6.9), based on an implementation from the University of Guelph.

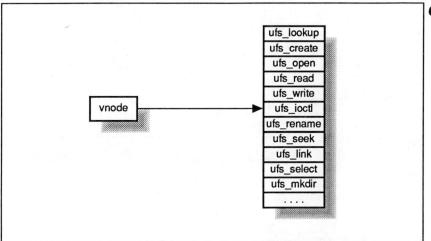

Vnodes represent files independently of file systems

A **vnode** is closely analogous to the inode (§6.5) of traditional UNIX file systems. It is a data structure in the virtual file system representing an individual file (in the broad sense, where a file could be, for example, a device or a pipe). It contains information about the file, and includes a pointer to the file system-specific routines that perform operations on the file itself. Every file in a mounted (§6.3) file system has a vnode associated with it.

When you create a new file, say, in the UFS file system, that file system allocates a vnode for the file and writes into the vnode a pointer to the routines that carry out file system-specific operations on the file. Thus, if you try to write to the file with the *write* system call, the vnode pointer for the write operation will refer to the *ufs_write* routine. If the file had been part of an S5 file system, then the vnode pointer would have selected a different write routine.

All of this is rather similar to the way that a *read* or *write* system call is "switched" to the read or write routine of a specific device driver by means of the *bdevsw* and *cdevsw* device switch tables (§5.2).

6.3

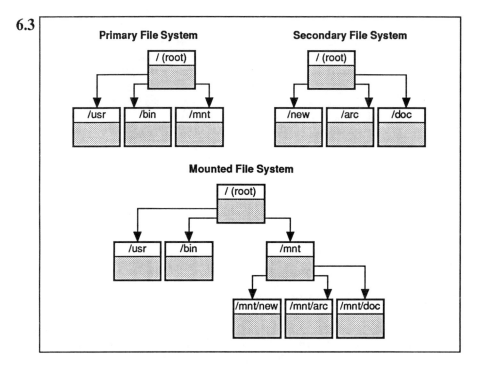

Mounting a file system

We have seen that each file is represented by a vnode containing a pointer to file system-specific routines enabling you to read or write the file. In the same way—but at a higher level of abstraction—an entire file system is represented by a data structure containing a pointer to operations related to the file system as a whole.

One of the things you can do with a file system as a whole is to **mount** it. From the standpoint of the user or system administrator, you mount a file system very much in the traditional UNIX fashion. This is shown in the illustration.

In one sense, there is always only one active file system—the **root file system**, into which any number of separate file systems have been "grafted", or mounted, at particular nodes. The resulting, composite file system looks to the user (for the most part) like a single, seamless entity. You can mount a file system upon a node of a previously mounted file system.

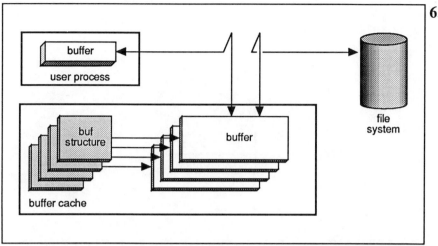

The operating system buffers file I/O

Traditional UNIX file I/O is normally synchronous from the standpoint of a user program. This is because an application must wait for a *read* or *write* call to be "effectively" completed before execution continues, and because only one I/O operation can be in progress for a particular device at any one time. However, the actual, low-level I/O for writes is asynchronous. This is due to the use of a **buffer cache**, almost universal in UNIX systems, including OSF/1.

When you read a file, the appropriate block of the file is read from disk into a buffer. Successive reads only require you to access the buffer, until you reach the end of the block, at which point a new block may be read into a buffer. Similarly with writes. If the file block to which you want to write is not currently in a buffer, it is read in. Then successive writes go only to the buffer, which is thereupon marked "dirty"—meaning that it has benn modified and must eventually be written back to disk. The actual disk write, however, may well occur later, after your application has already gone on to other activities.

The buffer cache has three main functions:

- to make possible concurrent I/O and computation within a UNIX process, by handling "real" I/O asynchronously

- to prevent an application from having to worry about calculating physical block boundaries in order to carry out efficient I/O—the operating system handles this by determining when to read in entire blocks

- to improve performance by reducing the frequency of physical I/O—a slow activity relative to CPU speed

6.5

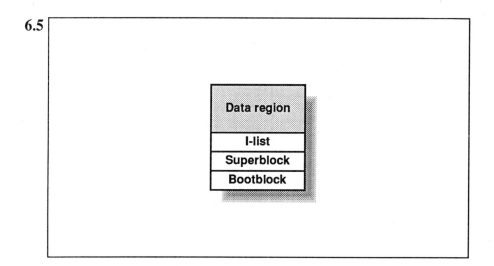

The structure of the S5 file system

S5 file system operations are not parallelized under OSF/1. The file system tends to be less efficient than UFS.

The figure illustrates the major elements of an S5 file system as it resides on disk. The **bootblock** is optionally available for containing a bootstrapping program. In this way the device containing the file system can be used as a boot device. However, while the boot block is still there, OSF/1 does not currently support booting from it.

The **superblock** describes the file system, and contains this information:

- the total size of the file system

- size of the inode list, or i-list. (See below)

- header of the list of free blocks—memory blocks available for allocation to files

- list of free inodes—that is, inodes available for the creation of new files

- modified and read-only flags

- number of free blocks and free inodes

The copy of the superblock resides in main memory so long as the file system is mounted.

The **i-list** is the portion of memory within the file system reserved for allocation of inodes, one per file. Each inode contains status information, pointers to data blocks in the file, permissions, and other information related to the corresponding file.

The **data region** is used for the actual data, or contents, of files. It normally occupies far the greatest part of the disk.

6.6

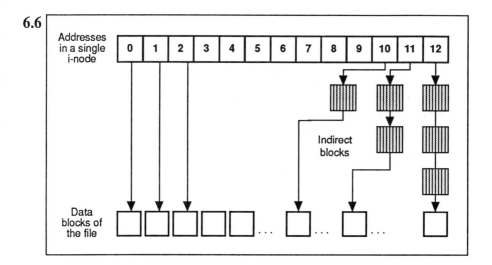

Inodes map the successive blocks of a file to physical blocks on disk

Each S5 inode that corresponds to an existing file contains 13 disk addresses pointing to the file's data blocks, or content. The first 10 of these point directly to the first 10 data blocks. The 11th address points to an entire block of additional addresses, if needed. (This block of addresses is known as an **indirect block**.) The 12th address points to a block of double-indirect addresses—that is, addresses that point to blocks of addresses. The 13th address points to a block of triple-indirect addresses.

The S5 file system allows blocks to be 512 bytes, 1K bytes, or 2K bytes in size. For 32-bit architectures, there is a limit on file size of 2 gigabytes.

This file system structure allows for **sparse files**—files with "holes" in them. It is possible, for example to take an empty file and write data at various offsets from the beginning of a file, even if nothing has ever been written to the intervening blocks. Thus, the first "real" data in a file might be pointed to by the 12th (double-indirect) disk address of the inode. The first 11 addresses would remain null, and the system can interpret null addresses as pointing to blocks filled with zeros. (In the case of a null indirect address, it can be taken to point to a block of null addresses.)

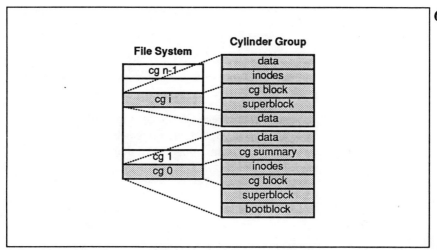

6.7

The structure of UFS

The UFS file system is divided into **cylinder groups** correlated with the physical layout of a disk. Each cylinder group contains a duplicate of the superblock, which in turn contains information about the layout of the file system. The super-block also remains in main memory so long as the file system is mounted.

A **cylinder summary**—maintained in the data section of cylinder 0—contains a summary of the available storage in each cylinder group. A copy of this summary resides in main memory while the file system is mounted.

The **cylinder group block** contains the free block map and all other allocation information. A copy resides in main memory as needed.

The successive blocks of data representing a file's content are mapped to physical disk blocks by a mechanism of direct and indirect addressing much like that described for S5 (§6.6), except that the block size is either 4K or 8K, and there are 15 disk addresses per inode instead of 13. (The first 12 are direct blocks. Again, due to address limitations of 32-bit architectures, maximum file size on such systems will be 2 gigabytes.)

Note that the superblock contains both static and dynamic information. The static information describes the layout of the entire file system and is essential to make sense out of the file system. The dynamic information describes the file system's current state, and can be computed from redundant information in the file system. If the static portion of the superblock is lost, the file system can no longer be used—which is why the superblock (or at least the static portion of it) is copied onto each cylinder group.

6.8

> **UFS:**
>
> - Filename components 255 bytes long
> - File blocks can be split into fragments
> - Optimizations reduce disk access time

Some features of UFS under OSF/1

The operating system components supporting UFS have been **parallelized**.

Unlike the S5 file system, which limits the individual components of a file path-name to 14 bytes, UFS allows pathname components to be **255 bytes long**, with the overall name restricted to 1023 bytes. This necessitates changes in the structure of the traditional UNIX file directory, including:

- the addition of information about the length of each filename

- the length of the overall directory entry for each file (which may contain free space at the end).

The large, 4K or 8K block size (fixed for each particular file system) invites inefficiency—the loss of usable disk space due to the fact that most files include unused space between the end of file data and the end of the last file block. UFS addresses this by allowing blocks to be split into **fragments**. These fragments may be assigned to different files.

However, there are restrictions: there can only be 1, 2, 4, or 8 fragments per block—a number that is fixed for any given file system; and such fragments can be assigned elsewhere only when they occur in the last block of a file.

UFS attempts to arrange a file's data blocks on disk not only so as to minimize wasted disk space, but also to **reduce disk access time.** This latter is accomplished by:

- placing inodes in the same cylinder group as their directory

- placing inodes for new directories in cylinder groups with maximum free space

- placing a file's directly addressed blocks in the inode's cylinder group

- placing indirectly addressed portions of a file in cylinder groups with maximum free space

Among the results of these strategies is a reduction in the amount of time the disk head must seek between the i-list and the data blocks of a file during reads and writes.

6.9

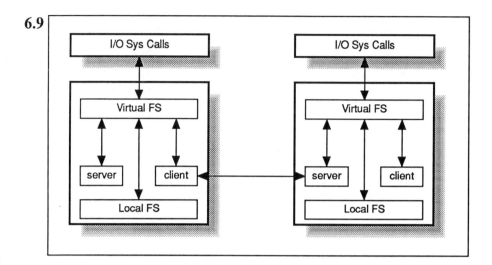

The NFS file system

The Network File system (NFS) supports remotely mounted file systems. When a remote file system is mounted on the local machine, its files become locally available in a manner that, to the end user and programmer, appears much the same as when one local file system is mounted (§6.3) upon another.

We do not provide an illustration here showing the "structure of the NFS file system"—as we did for the S5 and UFS file systems—because that would make no sense. NFS simply provides a mechanism by which you can mount remote file systems—whatever their type, as long as the systems on which they reside support NFS—and also by which you can offer up local file systems for mounting by remote machines. The "local file system" in the illustration on this page is not in and of itself an "NFS file system". It may, for example, be an S5 file system. It becomes an NFS file system only to the degree that it is accessed via a particular layer of file networking software. So NFS is a means by which specific file systems of whatever type can be made accessible between systems in a networked environment.

Of course, this relative transparency requires extensive software support. While local files are directly available, remote files are accessed through a client - server arrangement. This arrangement begins with the remote mount operation: when a user requests the mounting of a remote file system, the local machine sends an NFS remote procedure call (RPC) to the remote system. The *mountd* process of the remote server checks the requisite permissions (the */etc/exports* file contains a list of exportable file systems, together with the names of clients permitted to mount them), before returning a "file handle" for the root of the file system. The local system then uses this handle to mount (§6.3) the root of the remote file system at the designated node of the local file system.

Requests to access individual remote files follow a similar path. In examining the pathname, the local system (client-side) encounters the mount point, then passes the name to the remote server. The server returns a file handle identifying:

- the file system in which the file resides
- the file's inode number (§6.5)
- the file's inode generation number

The inode generation number—part of the file's inode—is necessary because the remote file may be deleted by another client, following which the same inode might be re-used for a newly created file. Since, in the latter case, the generation number will have been changed, and since the first client passes this number back to the server on subsequent access attempts, the server can tell whether to return a "stale file handler" error message back to the client.

The operating system components supporting NFS have been parallelized in OSF/1.

6.10

> **NFS servers are stateless**
>
> - Server crash recovery is trivial
> - Supported on different operating systems to enable file sharing
> - Do not support full UNIX semantics

Some features of NFS

Since servers do not try to maintain information about their clients, there is no need to recover such information after a crash. However, another implication of this "stateless" operation is that NFS semantics are not identical to UNIX semantics for certain I/O system calls.

For example, programmers commonly create temporary files by opening a new file and immediately unlinking it. So long as the file remains open, it exists, even though the link count is zero. (The "reference count" maintained in the vnode (§6.2) remains positive.) The file is automatically removed as soon as it is closed—typically upon program exit.

This sequence, however, will not work the same way with an NFS file. Since the server does not harbor state information, it can't know that the file remains open on the client side. Upon receiving the unlink request, the server immediately removes the file. To remedy this problem, the client automatically converts unlink requests to rename requests, changing the name of the file to some temporary name. The client issues an unlink request only when the application finally closes the file.

Another example of the difference between UNIX and NFS semantics arises when an application changes the access permissions of an open file. Access checks for UNIX files are performed only when the file is opened. Thus, if you successfully open a file for read-write access and subsequently change the permissions to read-only, write access to the already open file is still allowed. However, this would not be the case with an NFS file, since the NFS server must check permissions with each file access.

OSF/1 (and other UNIX implementations of NFS) provide a partial solution to this problem. The NFS client translates requests to the NFS server based on how a file was opened; the server allows read-write-execute access to the owner of a file regardless of the current permissions. Therefore, if the file was opened successfully for read-write access, the client allows both read and write calls—and the server implements them regardless of current permissions. But if the file is declared read-only, the client denies write requests.

A further difference between UNIX and NFS file system behavior results from the fact that NFS clients cache blocks from files provided by NFS servers. This means that processes on different machines do not necessarily have a consistent view of shared files (§6.11).

The great advantage of NFS, of course, is that it is supported under many different operating systems, and thereby allows file sharing to occur between otherwise incompatible systems. For example, PCs running MS-DOS can share files with UNIX machines, provided the systems on both sides have NFS. This kind of interchange is rapidly becoming essential in today's computing environments.

6.11

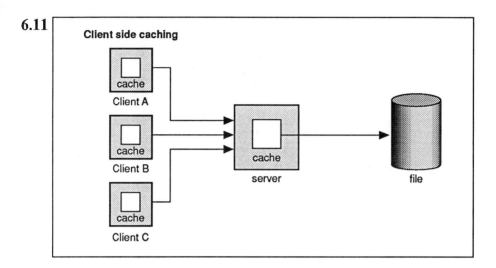

How to keep NFS client caches relatively consistent

Remote disk blocks are cached in the client's buffer cache. If multiple clients are using the same file, there may be a consistency problem. It is considered too expensive to keep the various caches fully consistent. However, an attempt is made to prevent too great an inconsistency.

In each NFS file node there is a copy of the associated remote file's attributes—the same information as is obtained from a *stat* system call, such as file modification time. Every time the attributes are fetched from the server, an expiration time of some number of seconds is set. If, when the file is next accessed, this time has not expired, it is assumed that locally cached blocks of the file remain valid. If, on the other hand, the time has expired, the new attributes must be obtained from the server and, if the file has been modified, the locally cached blocks are flushed. The cache is also flushed in response to *close, sync,* and *fsync* system calls.

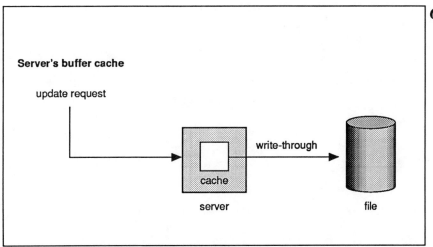

6.12

NFS servers perform automatic write-through

The server uses its buffer cache for handling client requests, but treats it as a write-through cache: a write request not only modifies the cache, but also causes the data to be written to the disk immediately. The request does not return until the disk-write completes.

This is consistent with the idea that NFS servers are stateless. If data were in the cache but not on the disk, clients could not be sure whether or not their requested changes to files were reflected in the file's actual data blocks on disk, since a system crash might have occurred between a cache write and a disk write.

Despite this need for synchronous I/O imposed by the requirement for reliability in remote file access, NFS makes available to the programmer many elements of asynchronous I/O. For example, client-side applications can obtain not only the current block of a remote file, but also additional blocks (read-ahead), without waiting for the additional blocks to arrive. They can also write to the locally cached blocks of a remote file without waiting for those blocks to be sent to the remote system. And even requests requiring remote access can be handled by means of special, asynchronous calls, which make use of separate threads of the operating system. Therefore, the application does not need to wait for the calls to complete before continuing its own processing.

7

OSF/1 ARCHITECTURE:
The Logical Volume Manager

IN THIS CHAPTER

- Features of the logical volume manager
- Logical and physical extents
- Disk mirroring
- Remapping bad sectors
- Flow of control
- Mirror consistency records
- Recovering from a crash

7.1

Logical volumes:

- may span multiple physical volumes
- may be mirrored on multiple physical volumes
- may span and shrink under the control of the administrator
- support software bad-sector remapping

Features of the logical volume manager

The logical volume manager (LVM) is a layer fitting between physical volumes and file systems. A **logical volume** looks and acts like a disk to the operating system, but can actually span multiple physical disks.

Disk mirroring is a means by which all writes to one logical volume are duplicated ("mirrored") by writes to either one or two additional volumes. The additional volumes are therefore duplicates of the first. This facilitates recovery in the event of damage to data on one of the volumes, and can improve system performance as well (§7.3).

File systems on UNIX usually correspond to a disk partition mounted in */dev*. Such file systems are therefore limited by the size restrictions of that disk. With the logical volume manager, however, a logical volume in */dev* can be mounted as the file system instead of an actual disk partition. Since **logical volumes can be dynamically resized** by the system administrator (§7.2), file systems are no longer restricted by the size of any one disk.

In addition, the logical volume manager can **detect and logically relocate bad sectors** on a disk (§7.4).

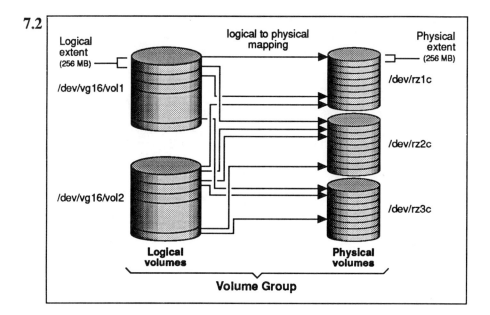

Logical and physical extents

Volume groups are groups containing both logical volumes and physical volumes. The logical volumes are divided into **logical extents,** and the physical volumes are divided into **physical extents.** The size of the logical and physical extents in a volume group is the same across the volume group.

Each logical extent is mapped to 1, 2, or 3 physical extents on physical volumes. When a single logical extent is mapped to either 2 or 3 physical extents, it is said to be **mirrored** (§7.3).

Logical volumes appear to be physical devices to most of the system, so they have a name as a special file in the /dev directory. By adding or removing logical extents on a logical volume, the size of the logical volume can be increased or decreased. Note, however, that when a logical volume is resized, the newfs command must be run on it to rebuild the file system, since file systems cannot be resized dynamically on OSF/1.

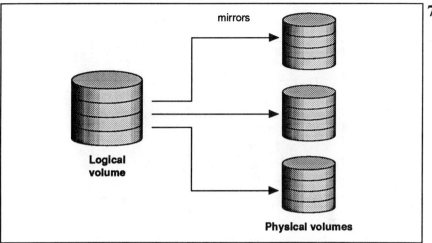

7.3

Disk mirroring

A single logical extent can be mapped to either 1, 2, or 3 physical extents. If a logical extent is mapped to 2 physical extents, it is said to be **singly mirrored**; if it is mapped to 3 physical extents, it is **doubly mirrored**. There are two motivations for disk mirroring: **speed** and **crash recovery**.

Mirroring can be used to speed read accesses to a logical volume. When a read request is made to a logical extent that is mirrored, the logical volume manager first determines which of the corresponding physical volumes is least active, and then translates it into a read of the physical extent on the least active physical volume.

This approach is most effective for logical volumes that are "read-mostly"—it is less effective for logical volumes that are written to frequently, due to the overhead of keeping all the mirrors updated. For a logical volume containing mostly binaries, however, disk mirroring can make a great improvement on the performance of that volume.

Perhaps the most important reason for disk mirroring is to provide enough redundancy to survive crashes. If a physical volume is lost, the data contained in it can be recovered from mirrored copies maintained in other physical volumes (§7.7).

7.4

> The LVM helps to remap bad sectors
>
> For hard errors:
> - the offending sector is remapped
> - the sector copied from a mirror if a mirror errors
>
> For soft errors:
> - the offending sector is verified and remapped if necessary

Remapping bad sectors

For mirrored volumes, the logical volume manager can fix newly-detected bad sectors by relocating the logical sector, reading the mirror, and writing the data into the relocated sector.

If a "soft" error occurs (i.e., an error that was detected and corrected by the disk controller), the data is rewritten from one of the mirrors, and write verification is requested from the disk drive. If the write fails or cannot be verified, the soft error is treated as a hard error.

If a "hard" error occurs, then the bad sector is relocated to a new sector. The new sector is taken from a pool of unused data sectors that the LVM reserves for this purpose. If the bad sector was mirrored, the LVM redirects any failed reads to another copy and uses the mirrored data to rewrite the new sector. Errors are not returned unless a hard error occurs on a read, and the corresponding physical extent is unmirrored.

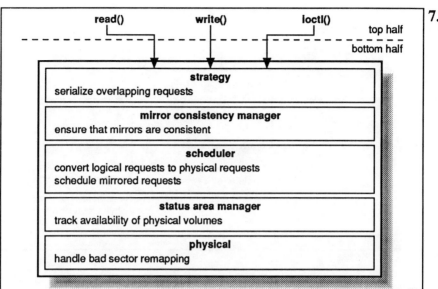

Flow of control

The logical volume manager device driver has a "top" half and a "bottom" half. The top half contains most of the entry points to the LVM, accessed via *read( )* and *write( )* system calls as well as LVM-specific *ioctl( )* commands. The *ioctl( )* commands can be used for a variety of functions, such as creating and deleting volume groups and configuring the LVM.

The bottom half of the LVM has five layers:

- The **strategy layer** serializes overlapping requests. It is used to synchronize requests with changes that are in progress at lower levels.

- The **mirror consistency manager** maintains the consistency of mirrors. It keeps a list of update operations in progress, so that it can regain consistency in the event of a crash.

- The **scheduler layer** is responsible for translating logical requests into physical requests. If the logical volume is mirrored, then each logical request may correspond to two or more physical requests.

- The **status area manager** makes sure that the physical volumes are available and keeps track of whether the physical extents are updated.

- The **physical layer** is responsible for bad sector relocation. It communicates directly with the physical device drivers and responds to disk errors by effecting the relocation of errors.

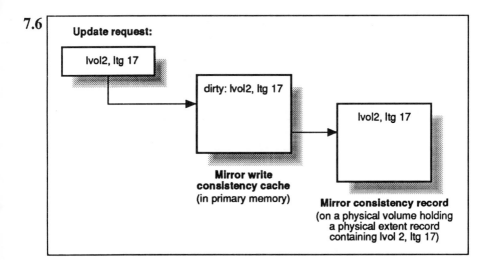

Mirror consistency records

The logical volume manager needs to make sure that when an update is requested to a logical extent, all physical mirrors of that logical extent are updated as well. Furthermore, the LVM needs to make sure that consistency is maintained when a crash occurs—if an update was in progress when a crash occurred, mirrored volumes may be out-of-sync.

The basic approach to maintaining consistency among mirrors is to keep a record on disk of the write operations currently in progress to mirrored extents. If a crash occurs, the operations that were in progress can be identified once the system is recovered, and the mirrors can be made consistent with one another. An up-to-date listing of updates in progress is kept in a **mirror consistency record** on disk.

The easiest way to achieve this would be to update the mirror consistency record before and after each disk write, but this would result in a very large overhead. Instead, the LVM uses a scheme in which each physical extent is divided into "logical track groups".

A **logical track group** (LTG) is defined to be 32 consecutive pages, where a "page" is the disk block size. Update operations in progress are represented by a data structure called the **mirror write consistency cache**, which contains 62 entries, each of which corresponds to a logical track group. Each active entry in the mirror write consistency cache is marked "clean" or "dirty", depending on whether an update operation is in progress.

Whenever a new entry is added to the mirror write consistency cache, the contents of the cache are copied to at least one of the corresponding physical volumes involved in the update, as a mirror consistency record. The mirror consistency record is therefore simply a recent copy of the cache on a physical volume.

The mirror consistency record lists update operations as being in progress for some time longer than they actually are in progress—the record entry is not reused when there is no outstanding I/O, but remains until the logical volume is closed. This method results in a longer crash recovery procedure, but saves time in recording updates.

7.7

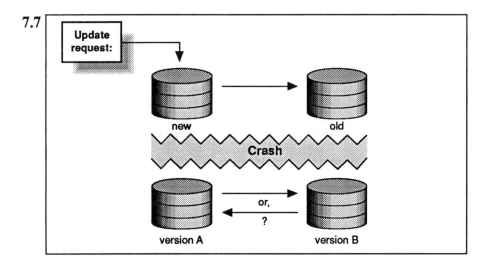

Recovering from a crash

When a crash occurs, the mirror consistency manager is responsible for restoring consistency using the mirror consistency records saved on disk.

Crash recovery begins with locating the most recent mirror consistency record, which contains a list of logical track groups that were being modified. For each logical track group on the list, the mirror consistency manager chooses one mirror arbitrarily and copies its tracks onto each of the other mirrors. Data may not be fully updated to the time immediately before the crash, but it is guaranteed to be consistent across mirrors.

Another possible problem, however, is that a physical volume may become unavailable (e.g., because of controller or media failures). If a doubly-mirrored volume was lost in a crash, then it is unknown whether or not it contained the most recent mirror consistency record.

In this situation, OSF/1 assumes the worst case (with the explicit permission of the operator): that every logical track group on the volume was being modified at the time of the crash, so all associated mirrors may be inconsistent. All physical extents of this volume are therefore marked "dirty" in the mirror write consistency cache, and all logical extents that were double-mirrored are resynchronized by copying one of the accessible physical extents to the other (the second physical extent is also marked "dirty"). Note that if the logical extent was singly-mirrored, there is no consistency problem to resolve, since only one accessible physical extent remains.

8

OSF/1 ARCHITECTURE:

Security

IN THIS CHAPTER

- The Rainbow Series

- Orange Book divisions

- Standard UNIX systems are C1-compliant

- C2 requires auditing

- C2 enables Access Control Lists on OSF/1 (a B3 feature)

- C2 enables Least Privilege on OSF/1 (a B2 feature)

- B1 systems have Mandatory Access Control

- B2 and higher (not supported by OSF/1)

8.1

The **Rainbow Series** is a set of documents outlining government specifications on computer security.

The **Orange Book** contains government security requirements for standalone systems.

The Rainbow Series

As in any industry, UNIX vendors need to attend to their customers' needs. This is especially true if your biggest customer is the U.S. Government.

One of the most critical requirements of many Government contracts is that a system be "secure". In 1983, the Department of Defense defined what "security" means for computers, and so began the **Rainbow Series**. The first book was the **Orange Book**, written in 1983 and updated in 1985. Other colors of the rainbow are Red, Purple, Yellow, etc.—at this writing, there are roughly 20 in all.

The Government specification we're most concerned with is the Orange Book, a.k.a. the "Department of Defense Trusted Computer System Evaluation Criteria", which concerns itself strictly with standalone systems.

Since many readers may not be familiar with security concepts and terminology, this chapter provides an outline of the specifications detailed in the Orange Book as well as discussion of OSF's security offering.

8.2

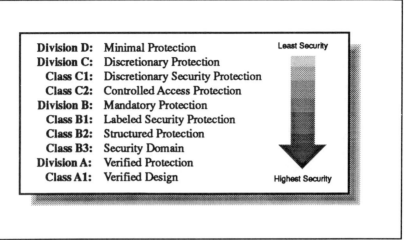

Division D:	Minimal Protection	Least Security
Division C:	Discretionary Protection	
Class C1:	Discretionary Security Protection	
Class C2:	Controlled Access Protection	
Division B:	Mandatory Protection	
Class B1:	Labeled Security Protection	
Class B2:	Structured Protection	
Class B3:	Security Domain	
Division A:	Verified Protection	
Class A1:	Verified Design	Highest Security

Orange Book divisions

The Orange Book defines four general **divisions** from A to D, with A being the most secure and D being the least. In addition, Division C is separated into two classes, and Division B is divided into three classes. Each level includes all the functionality of each previous level—so, for example, a class B2 system includes all the functionality of a B1 system as well as all the functionality of all C-class systems.

Secure systems are inherently slower than non-secure systems. Therefore, each customer should take the time to determine exactly what level of security is most appropriate to purchase for their needs. Note, however, that many federal government requisitions already specify particular security levels, and many will soon be requiring B1 certification.

The words **subject** and **object** are used often in security discussions. In most cases, if you substitute the words "user" and "file", you'll be all right. "Subjects" actually correspond not just to users, but to their processes as well—that is, anything that might request access an object. "Objects" correspond to files and directories, i.e., items that need to be protected against access by unauthorized subjects. Security, then, simply boils down to determining whether subjects have permission to access or change objects.

This chapter describes each of the Orange Book levels in sequence, but please note that what OSF/1 offers goes beyond the requirements at each level. Since the emphasis of this book is OSF/1, we list all features at the level at which OSF/1 makes them accessible. In particular:

- Access Control Lists" (§8.5) are provided at the C2 level for OSF/1, but are not required by the Orange Book until level B3.

- Least Privilege (§8.6) is provided partially at the C2 level for OSF/1, and is fully supported at the B1 level. The Orange Book does not require Least Privilege to be implemented until level B2.

8.3

> UNIX systems are C1 compliant.
> **Discretionary Access Control** (DAC) allows
> users to restrict access to their data (as with
> chmod(1)).

Standard UNIX systems are C1-compliant

Lowest on the security totem pole is **Division D**. Systems with a "D" rating have been evaluated and have flunked.

C1 systems must provide controls for protecting private information and for preventing others from destroying data by accident. This is called **Discretionary Access Control**, or DAC. "Discretionary" means that the file owner can decide, at his or her own discretion, whether to share a file with others. UNIX file access modes already do this to some extent—by making a file read/write only to the owner, we can prevent others from accessing its contents.

Almost any UNIX system is therefore already C1-compliant—meaning that it offers all the features of a C1 system, although it hasn't been officially certified as such. In addition, vendors have the option of compiling OSF/1 to comply with either C2 or B1 specifications. (With the exception of auditing, end users cannot adapt the security configuration on their system once it is shipped.)

Note that a system can be compliant at a certain level without being certified. To get the government stamp of approval, platforms need to go through a lengthy, formal evaluation process. Operating systems alone (e.g., UNIX) cannot be certified—only operating systems on a particular architecture with a given set of options can be granted government certification.

8.4

OSF/1 supplies **auditing procedures** for C2 compliance
- Auditing makes users accountable for their actions
- The level of auditing can be changed dynamically during run-time of the system

C2 requires auditing

In addition to the requirements for C1, **C2 systems** require the ability to to make users individually accountable for their actions. This requires authenticating logins with strict password guidelines* and auditing individual user actions. UNIX systems already perform minimal auditing—for example, the console messages that result when someone runs the *su* command. With more complete auditing, however, administrators can track logins and privileged system calls. This could be used, for example, to determine when files are opened, closed, removed, or renamed.

Note that although most other aspects of the security configuration for a system are determined when the operating system is compiled, the level of auditing can be chosen at run time. An administrator can reduce the amount of auditing when the system is overloaded, or can increase it when suspicious activities are on the rise. The administrator can choose which events should be audited by user ID or group ID. On systems with Mandatory Access Control (§8.7) enabled (B1 systems and up), events can also be selected for auditing according to their sensitivity level.

---

* OSF/1 follows the rules for password authentication as defined by the DoD's *Password Management Guideline*, a.k.a. "The Green Book".

8.5

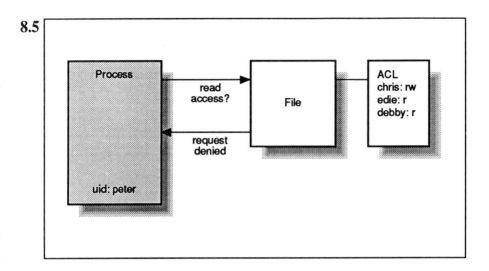

C2 enables Access Control Lists on OSF/1 (a B3 feature)

In OSF/1, Discretionary Access Control can be extended to include **Access Control Lists** (ACLs), a feature that is actually required only on B3 systems.

On traditional UNIX systems, you can restrict access to a file to a selected few only by juggling its **rwx** file permissions with the *chmod* command, and using *chgrp* to determine which group should have group access. Consequently, many sites end up with dozens of groups, each for a different type of access. However, it often occurs that someone needs access to a particular file, but doesn't need to be in its group. Not uncommonly, the "solution" is to make the file accessible to everyone and be done with it. A similar complication arises when one wants to prevent access by a particular user.

Access Control Lists are designed to remedy those situations. With Access Control Lists, each file or directory can have an associated list of users with specific access rights. This allows the owner to "fine-tune" access to a file.

With ACLs, you can add a single user to the Access Control List for a file, without having to make the file open to the world or to an entire group. You can also exclude a single user at your discretion.

8.6

Authorizations and Privileges

- **command authorizations** restrict certain subsystems and commands to designated users
- **kernel authorizations** restrict rights at the operating system level

Kernel authorizations given to programs or processes are called **privileges**.

C2 enables Least Privilege on OSF/1 (a B2 feature)

At the C2 level on OSF/1, **root** permission has been divided into a large number of very specific authorizations and privileges, designed to work together to define "least privilege" for a given process. "Least privilege" is actually not required until B2, according to the Orange Book.

By **least privilege**, we mean that rather than having the all-or-nothing scheme that is traditional to UNIX systems (i.e., you're either a mere mortal or Superuser, with nothing in between), multiple levels of privilege are supplied. Each privileged user is given only the fewest privileges necessary for a particular job, with those privileges extending over the shortest time possible. In this scheme, a user might attain permission to stop and restart the print spooler, but would not have permission to create accounts for new users.

The difference between authorizations and privileges in OSF/1 is a bit murky. Basically, there are two kinds of authorizations, **kernel authorizations** and **command authorizations**. Kernel authorizations give rights to the operating system, and command authorizations give rights to particular commands. When kernel authorizations are given to a program or process, they are called **privileges**.

An example of a kernel authorization is the **chown** authorization, which allows a user to change the ownership of a file to another user. Examples of command authorizations are the **printqueue** authorization, which allows you to see jobs other than your own on the printer queue, and the **lp** authorization, which allows a user to configure the *lp* subsystem.

Trusted applications are applications that are guaranteed to use "least privilege" at all times. For writing trusted applications, OSF/1 supplies a Trusted Application Programming Interface (TAPI). With TAPI, programs can switch privilege levels during execution, so that the entire program does not need to keep up a particular privilege level just to perform a single system call.

Although authorizations and privileges are enabled at the C2 level for an OSF/1 system, privileges are extended to executable files only at the B1 level of security.

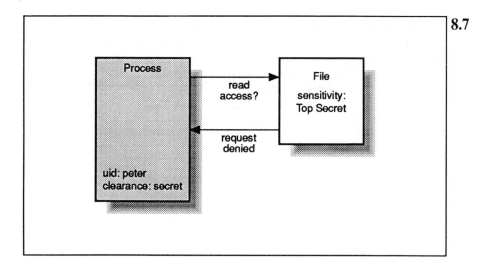

8.7

B1 systems have Mandatory Access Control

Access Control Lists clearly make it easier for users to control access to their files. In a really secure environment, however, it isn't enough—frankly, access control shouldn't have to be maintained entirely by the user. This makes the system harder to use and also leaves a lot of room for user error. To qualify for **B1 security**, a system must provide **data labeling** and **Mandatory Access Control** (MAC) over named processes and files.

In Mandatory Access Control, every subject in the system has a security level (called a **clearance**) and every object has a **sensitivity label**. By comparing the user's clearance with the file's sensitivity label, the system decides whether the user is allowed to access the file. "Mandatory" means that the system mandates access rules. A file owner can't decide to share a file that is governed by Mandatory Access Control, as one can with Discretionary Access Control.

Mandatory Access Control also protects against many types of system break-in or vandalism. Many break-ins are engineered by designing a program which, if run by a highly-cleared user, alters data on a lower level of sensitivity. The rule enforced by Mandatory Access Control is that you can read your level or lower, and you can write to your level or higher. This seems bizarre, but the logic behind it is consistent: since you cannot read a higher level, you cannot modify the data but only append to it. So a user with "Secret" clearance might be able to write an entry into a "Top Secret" log file, but wouldn't be able to read other entries in that log file. On the other hand, a user with "Secret" clearance might be able to read documents of lower sensitivity, but would not be able to copy Secret material into them.

Note that labeling and Mandatory Access Control can also be configured to apply to output devices, so restricted documents can't be printed out on public printers or copied onto floppy disks.

In addition, although authorizations and privileges are defined on the C2 level in OSF/1, it is not until the B1 level that they are extended to include privileges on executable files.

8.8

> **B2 systems require:**
> - assurance and a formal security model
> - DAC and MAC extended to all models
> - "least privilege"
>
> **B3 systems require:**
> - trusted recovery
> - support of security administrator
> - ACLs
> - reference monitor concept
>
> **A1 systems require** proof and trusted distribution

B2 and higher (not supported by OSF/1)

B2 and higher systems don't offer too many more specific security features beyond B1, but they require much more rigorous design, testing, and proof of security, known as **assurance**. Although OSF/1 does not supply the ability to be configured to any level above B1, we supply a brief description of those levels to complete our outline of the Orange Book guidelines.

B2 systems extend the discretionary and mandatory access controls of B1 to all objects in the system, including devices. Configuration management and documentation thereof is required as a **formal security model**, a mathematical statement of the system's security policy. B2 systems also require **least privilege**, which is enabled in OSF/1 as low as the C2 level.

B3 systems add a few features—like **trusted recovery**, support of a separate security administrator, and additional discretionary access controls (such as ACLs, which are enabled at the C2 level in OSF/1). But the main difference between B3 and less secure systems is the far more rigorous system design and assurance requirements. The central security kernel of the system, known as the Trusted Computing Base (TCB), must be rigorously designed, fundamentally very simple, and proven largely with mathematical means to be tamperproof and impossible to bypass. This is called the **reference monitor concept**.

For a system to be certified as **A1**, there must be a formal analysis and mathematical proof that the system design matches the system's security policy and its design specifications. The only specific feature added at the A1 level is **trusted distribution**, which ensures the security of the system while it's being shipped from the vendor to the customer.

9

PROGRAMMING UNDER OSF/1:

The Environment

IN THIS CHAPTER

- OSF/1 provides the UNIX programming tools
- Portability and compatibility
- Compiler, assembler, and linker

	9.1

UNIX programming environment
- Powerful tools
- Open approach
- The traditional strength of UNIX

OSF/1 provides the UNIX programming tools

Much of the power and reputation of UNIX has stemmed from its accumulated programming tools and the system environment that supports those tools. Rather than produce large, monolithic, "vertically integrated" utilities, the logic of UNIX has encouraged the development of numerous, well-focused tools that lend themselves in a mix-and-match way to the formation of programming environments custom-tailored to individual projects. Furthermore, the relatively "open" nature of UNIX has led to a massive channeling of programmer energy and ingenuity into the ongoing refinement of old tools and development of new tools.

OSF/1 offers the programming environment features of both System V (AT&T) and BSD (Berkeley) UNIX. It has a major impact on the programmer's world by virtue of its incorporation of standards and emphasis on portability. It includes the C shell, Bourne shell, and Korn shell. Its command set strives to convey the "look and feel" expected by both BSD and System V UNIX users. And it includes a range of enhanced tools from the Free Software Foundation—the GNU C compiler, assembler, linker, and debugger, as well as the GNU *emacs* editor. (These Free Software Foundation tools are not actually on the OSF/1 tape, but come free on a separate tape, without licensing requirements. They are not officially supported by OSF.)

Note, finally, that vendors supplying OSF/1 to their customers will very likely support their own customary or proprietary program development software in addition to, or instead of, the native OSF/1 capabilities. For example, while OSF makes the GNU compiler available to vendors, most vendors will supply their own compilers, suitable for the OSF/1 environment.

The familiar and standard UNIX programming tools do not require description here. However, it can be instructive to see even the most abbreviated summary of these utilities, which we therefore list here. Some of the more distinctive tools will receive further treatment in the following sections. (The number in parentheses following the name of a utility refers in the traditional manner to the section of the UNIX reference documentation in which a description of the utility can be found.)

Assembling, compiling, linking

gas(1)   GNU assembler. Compiles assembly language source files into binary files, and creates formatted listings of these files. Not officially supported by OSF.

/lib/cpp   C pre-processor. It expands macros, incorporates include files, and reckons with conditional compilation switches. This is run automatically by the C compiler, but you can also run it manually to see what your source file looks like after pre-processing.

gcc(1)   GNU C compiler. Compiles C-language source files into binary files. Optionally invokes *gld* upon those files. Can also output assembly language source files corresponding to the C sources. Not officially supported by OSF.

gld(1)   GNU linker. Links binary files into executable programs in the traditional way. Enhancements allow it to support shared libraries and dynamic loading. Not officially supported by OSF.

lint(1)   Analyzes C programs and reports undesirable programming practices as well as errors. By requiring all programs to pass *lint* inspection, project managers can guarantee that certain minimal programming standards are met throughout the project.

strip(1)   Removes symbols and relocation bits from binary files. This impairs the usefulness of debuggers, but saves space once a program has been successfully debugged.

Program debugging

adb(1)   Traditional UNIX debugger, offering relatively low-level access to program code, data, and register contents. Not officially supported by OSF.

gdb(1)   GNU debugger. General-purpose debugging. Enhancements allow debugging of multi-threaded applications and shared libraries. Not officially supported by OSF.

monitor(3)   A high-level interface to *profil(2)*. The **–p** switch of *cc(1)* results in automatic calls to *monitor*, and *prof(1)* reports the results of such monitoring. (Available in release 1.1.)

prof(1)   Produces an execution profile of a program, using data taken from the profile created when you compile with the **–p** option of *cc(1)*. (Available in release 1.1.)

profil(2)   Enables run-time execution profiling and gathers data for the profile. *monitor(3)* is a somewhat higher-level interface to *profil*. The **–p** option of *cc(1)* automatically causes *monitor* to be called. (Available in release 1.1.)

ptrace(2)   Enables one process to control the execution of a second process, examining and changing its core image. This is used primarily for breakpoint debugging.

Managing program libraries

ar(1)   Creates and maintains groups of executable modules organized into libraries (archives).

lorder(1)   Finds an ordering relation for the modules in a library by showing which modules contain reference to which others. By combining *lorder* with *tsort(1)*, you can order a library so that the linker (*gld*) is guaranteed to resolve all symbolic references in a single pass.

ranlib(1)   Converts libraries of executable modules to a form that can be linked more efficiently. *ranlib* accomplishes this by placing a symbolic table of contents at the beginning of the library.

tsort(1)   Topological sorting utility, used in conjunction with *lorder(1)*.

Managing software projects.

make(1)   Maintains, updates, and regenerates groups of programs. It is an extremely powerful and widely distributed tool for automatically maintaining complex programs in a consistent and updated state as individual modules are added, modified, and deleted. OSF/1's *make* is not parallelized in release 1.0, but is scheduled for parallelization in 1.1.

sccs(1)   Source code control system. Provides version control of program source files, enabling software developers to maintain and track successive versions and variants of large, complex products consisting of numerous individual modules.

Automatic program generation

lex(1)　　　Generates programs that perform lexical analysis upon their input. *lex* reads a specification file defining the symbol patterns to look for, and creates a C-language routine. This routine analyzes its input and identifies the designated patterns, or "tokens". *lex* can be used in generating the lexical analysis portion of a compiler.

yacc(1)　　　Generates programs that parse their input. That is, they recognize syntactical structures—such as sentences in ordinary language, or statements in programs—and invoke appropriate blocks of user-supplied code whenever such structures are encountered. *yacc* can be used in generating the parser portion of a compiler, and can take the output of *lex(1)* as its input.

Creating and editing source files

vi(1), emacs(1)

　　　Screen-oriented text editors. One of the tools obtained from the Free Software Foundation, *emacs* is not officially supported.

awk(1)　　　Scans its input for lines matching any of a set of specified patterns. Upon finding a pattern, *awk* carries out user-supplied instructions. This makes it easy, for example, to extract particular information from files containing organized information, and to perform trans-formations on certain fields of such a file.

cb(1)　　　Formats and "beautifies" C-language programs. This can contribute toward the maintenance of a common programming style within a large project.

cflow(1)　　　Analyzes C, yacc, lex, and assembler source files, as well as object files, and generates a chart of all external references in the files. Symbol names, data types, line numbers where symbol references and definitions are found, and nesting information are all provided.

csplit(1)　　　Splits a large C-language (or other text) file into smaller files for more convenient editing.

ctags(1)　　　Creates a tags file for use with *vi(1)*. The file contains a set of func-tion names and corresponding search strings for a set of C-language source files. This enables you to move rapidly to any given function declaration when you are editing any of the source files.

diff(1)　　　Compares two files, showing line-by-line differences between them. This is extremely useful for determining what changes have been made in particular revisions of source files.

mkstr(1)   Removes error strings from C source files into a separate error file, and massages the source files so that the error messages will be read from the separate file. This reduces the size of programs containing many error messages, and also cuts down on system overhead during execution of the programs.

sed(1)   Stream editor. A non-interactive editor with commands similar to a subset of *vi(1)* commands, it allows you to perform standard editing functions on your source and project files from within scripts or Makefiles.

xstr(1)   Extracts strings from C programs in order to implement shared strings. *xstr* replaces all string constants in a set of source files with references to a new, shared array of string definitions that the utility creates. This array is placed in a separate source file.

Miscellaneous

file(1)   Determines the nature of the specified files. For example, it reports whether a file is C-language source, assembly language, binary, a source file for the *troff* text formatter, and so on. In the case of binary files, it tells which of various binary formats is represented.

find(1)   Locates files anywhere in a file system, based on many possible criteria, such as file name, file type, owner, permissions, time of last modification, and so on. It allows you to act on the "found" files by executing arbitrary shell commands.

grep(1)   Searches for strings in files. Search strings can be defined in terms of typical UNIX "regular expressions", allowing the use of various wildcard and other special characters.

nm(1)   Prints a list of symbols in the object modules or libraries specified as arguments. Various information about the symbols is given, such as whether or not they are defined in the object module where they occur.

od(1)   Allows you to read binary files. The files can be displayed according to many options: by byte, short word, or long word; and with data displayed in the form of octal, decimal or hexidecimal numbers, or as ASCII characters. This command also allows you to search for certain character sequences in binary files.

size(1)   Lists the size of the various segments of a binary file.

strings(1)   Finds all the ASCII strings in a binary file. This includes text like file names, error messages, *printf* strings, and so on. Among many other things, you can use the utility to help identify random binary files.

what(1)   Used in conjunction with *sccs(1)*, this command prints out information about the version number and derivation of all the modules comprising an executable file.

9.2

Source code compatibility

- System V, Release 3 (SVID-2)
- 4.3 BSD
- Environmental variable for switching
  between SVR3 and 4.3 BSD

Portability and compatibility

Translated into practical terms, the OSF/1 emphasis on standards and portability
means **source code compatibility**. That is, you can take a program that adheres
to the various standards (§1.5) OSF/1 supports, re-compile and re-link it, and it
will run under OSF/1. (This will not be true, however, if your program also
makes use of non-standard, vendor-added features not included in OSF/1.)

More particularly, programs that run on System V, Release 3 and 4.3BSD should
be compatible, on the source file level, with OSF/1.

However, there are minor incompatibilities between those two operating systems
that, under some circumstances, you must carefully negotiate. For example, some
C library (*libc*) functions have different semantics under System V, Release 3,
and 4.3BSD. In such cases OSF/1 typically uses the System V behavior as the
default. To get BSD behavior, you would then set the BSD environmental variable. This does two things:

- it passes the **–D_BSD** option to the C compiler, causing it to read in the
  appropriate BSD header files

- it passes the **–lbsd** option to the linker, causing it to link in the BSD version of
  libc

More generally, OSF arbitrates between competing standards and selects defaults according to a hierarchy of preference:

International standards (e.g., ISO standards)

National standards (e.g., IEEE standards)

Industry specifications (e.g., X/Open's XPG)

Vendor specifications (e.g., SVID, BSD)

The Application Environment Specification (volume governing operating system programming interfaces) is OSF's definitive statement on these issues, covering all OSF/1 interfaces and their relation to existing standards.

Here's a brief checklist for ensuring portability:

1. Always adhere to supported **standards**.

2. Don't make assumptions about **hardware-related features** such as byte order, integer size, or instruction speed.

3. Be aware of **entry point conflicts**. There are certain entry points in the libraries and the operating system that have the same names but different calling sequences or argument types.

4. Do not look directly at kernel data structures, such as */dev/kmem* or the *u_task* and *u_thread* structures (§2.3).

5. Understand that the "standard" location for files in the file system is largely the same as for System V, Release 4.

Programs developed on your current platform do not necessarily need to be re-compiled under OSF/1 on the same platform. If your compiler produced object files in one of the standard formats supported by OSF/1 (initially COFF and OSF/ROSE), then it may be that those files can be executed without further change. However, no such binary compatibility is guaranteed by OSF, since your platform vendor is free to modify or enhance the operating system further. In general, binary compatibility is a system vendor issue, not an OSF issue. OSF has simply tried to make it possible for vendors to offer binary compatibility if they wish to do so.

One thing is sure, however: existing binaries will not be able to take advantage of the loader's ability to manage such things as shared libraries (§10.4) and dynamic loading (§10.8). For that, you will need to re-compile and re-link using either OSF's *gcc* and *gld*, or the compiler and linker provided by your system vendor.

9.3

Modified GNU program development tools

New Features:

- Shared libraries
- Position-independent code
- OSF/ROSE binary file format
- Library "packages"—different ways to access the same library
- Debugging of multi-threaded programs

Compiler, assembler, and linker

The compiler (*gcc*), assembler (*gas*), and linker (*gld*)—together with the debugger (*gdb*) and an editor (*emacs*)—are all derived from the Free Software Foundation's "GNU" software. The terms of the license require OSF to distribute it separately from the rest of the operating system, without charge. Many vendors who adopt OSF/1 will undoubtedly produce compilers, assemblers, linkers, and debuggers of their own.

The GNU compiler and related tools are being modified by OSF to support a number of special features, some of which may not be available until release 1.1 or beyond:

Shared libraries. All running processes can share a single, memory-resident copy of a library routine.

Position-independent code. When a module containing such code is executed, the loader is free to choose where to place it in memory, adjusting all memory references within the module as necessary.

Special placement of **static data** so that it can be efficiently accessed.

To help make these capabilities possible, the assembler responds to several new pseudo-ops (that is, operations that are used in managing the creation of binary modules without resulting directly in machine code):

.sect   Specifies a new type of program section for holding transfer information and global variables.

.setpic   Tells the assembler to create position-independent code—for example, by using relative instead of absolute branches.

.dt   Facilitates placement of static data in the object module.

.dptr   Identifies external references that need not be resolved until load time, thus supporting the use of shared libraries.

The assembler generates object files in OSF/ROSE format.

The OSF-modified linker (*gld*) works closely with the compiler and assembler to support position-independent code. It can link modules into shared libraries, and links programs against existing shared libraries.

The linker also reckons with the notion of **packages** (§10.9). A package is a set of externally visible names for selected modules of a library. For example, suppose a single library contained both XTI and TLI transport layer modules. Two packages might be defined over that library, so that—linking to the correct package—a program could gain access to the modules for the desired protocol. To switch to the other protocol would require only linking to a different package, not changing the names of library calls in the source code.

Note that the linker is still able to link code from existing libraries that do not support position-independent code.

Finally, the debugger (*gdb*) has also been modified so as to deal with multi-threaded programs and shared libraries. Another new feature allows the debugger to carry out dynamic searches of a program's symbol table. By this means you can locate the symbolic name associated with a given address or value. Of course, *gdb* has been made to recognize the OSF/ROSE binary format.

See Chapter 10 for a detailed discussion of the OSF/1 **loader**.

10

PROGRAMMING UNDER OSF/1:
The Loader

IN THIS CHAPTER

- Symbol definitions and symbol references
- Resolving external references
- Relocation
- Shared libraries
- The run-time loader
- Multiple format support
- Extensions to exec()
- Dynamic loading and unloading
- Packages
- Package tables
- Using the private package table

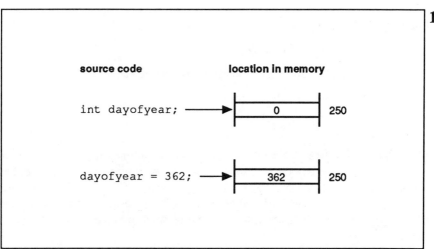

Symbol definitions and symbol references

Before we discuss linking and loading under OSF/1, let's backtrack a bit and identify the roles of the linker and loader on traditional UNIX systems.

Programs contain symbol definitions and symbol references. For example, the C language declaration:

```
int dayofyear;
```

defines a symbol called dayofyear, reserving a memory location (say, location 250) to contain the value associated with the symbol. At program initialization this value may be 0, and when the variable is explicitly assigned a value, the new value is placed at the address dayofyear (as seen in the figure).

Given such a definition, another routine in a separate module of the program might refer to this same symbol with the declaration:

```
extern int dayofyear;
```

This sort of "external" declaration does *not* result in allocation of memory to store a value, but simply associates the symbol, dayofyear, with the symbol definition given in the first routine. By examining both routines together, the linker determines that the reference in the second routine is to the memory location for dayofyear defined in the first routine.

Similarly, the symbol reference:

```
date = getdayofmonth();
```

requires a definition of the subroutine called getdayofmonth():

```
int getdayofmonth() {
...
}
```

This definition can be in the same module, in a different module, or in an **archive** of modules—such as a library. When the program is "linked", the linker searches for the definition of the getdayofmonth() routine. If it is found in any of the linked modules or libraries, the address of the subroutine definition becomes the address to which the program transfers control when getdayofmonth() is called.

In general, symbol definitions result in allocation of memory to hold certain contents, and symbol references refer to the associated memory addresses. The **linker** and the **loader** work together to match symbols with their definitions, transparent to the programmer and user.

The roles of the linker and loader in UNIX program generation have always been easily confused. In what we call "traditional UNIX", the program *ld* performed both functions at once, and was called the "linker/loader" or "linking loader". More confusion arose from the fact that run time is often called "load time", since programs are "loaded" into memory at that stage. In OSF/1, the roles of the linker and loader have become more distinct.

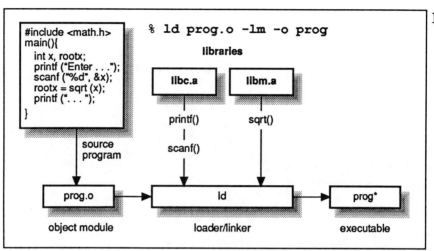

```
% ld prog.o -lm -o prog
```

10.2

Resolving external references

Most large programs are broken into smaller, discrete source modules, which are compiled separately into object modules and then linked together into a single executable file.

As the linker processes each module, it comes to symbol definitions and symbol references, as described in the previous section. Some of these references may not be previously defined. References that are undefined are known as **unresolved references.** They are also called **external references,** since they refer to symbols defined in other modules. A common example of an external reference is a reference to a function that resides in one of the system libraries.

The traditional "linking loader" in UNIX, *ld*, would **resolve** each external reference when it came to its definition. It would accomplish this by keeping track of each external reference and the address where it was called. If the definition of an external reference was found in one of the system libraries, the linker *ld* would copy the module containing the definition into the program, and then fill in the address of the definition within that module for all references. In this way, the reference was **resolved.**

For example, for each time the *printf( )* function was called, *ld* would enter the symbol name and calling address into an internal table. When the definition of *printf( )* was found in the *stdio* library, its module would be copied to the executable file, and the address of the *printf( )* definition within that copy would be supplied for each *printf( )* reference. Each call to *printf( )* thus becomes a transfer to whatever address the *printf( )* function was copied to.

10.3

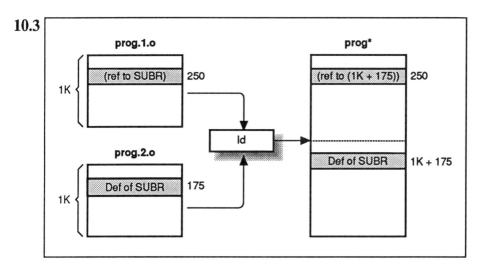

Relocation

The other important function that the "linking loader" *ld* traditionally performed was **relocation**. Simplifying greatly, suppose a program is compiled into two object modules, each occupying exactly 1K of memory. The linker builds a single, executable file from the two modules. If getdayofmonth() is referred to at address 250 of the first module, and if its declaration in the second module results in allocation of memory for the variable at location 175 of the second module—and if, finally, the linker places the second module immediately after the first in the executable file—then the linker must make sure that the reference to getdayofmonth() at address 250 of the new file refers to memory address (1K + 175) of the executable file.

This determination of the "real" addresses in memory for a fully linked executable—that is, addresses relative to the actual beginning of the program and not just to the beginning of the current object module—is called **relocation**. When a program is fully relocated, all program addresses become fixed and static, or **bound**, and the program is ready to execute as soon as it is **loaded** from secondary memory into system virtual memory (§4.1) at address 0.

All of this describes a fairly conventional programming environment. In OSF/1, however, much of the function of *ld* which has been described here has been removed from the formal "linking" process. Instead, the function of *ld* has been separated into a two-step process. The linker still creates the executable file, but symbol resolution and relocation can now be partially delayed until run time, resulting in more flexibility and support for shared libraries. At that time, the **run-time loader** is called (§10.5).

10.4

Shared libraries are supported in OSF/1
- a single copy of each library module is
  used by all programs
- saves disk space
- saves processing time

Shared libraries

Consider a program with all external symbols resolved. Now consider the disad-
vantages associated with it.

Imagine twenty such programs running at once, each of which calls *printf( )* at
least once. If each of these programs has its own copy of *printf( )*, then there are
altogether twenty copies for the operating system to manage in memory. When
you consider how many other routines are being duplicated across the system, it's
clear that performance is taking a beating—not to mention the waste of disk
space storing executables containing duplicate routines.

In order to prevent unnecessary duplication of routines, **shared libraries** were
conceived, in which single copies of library modules become available for all
programs to use. (OSF/1 is among many recent versions of UNIX that support
shared libraries.)

OSF/1 pre-relocates shared libraries to reserved positions. What this means is
that the libraries are assigned to a fixed location in the address space. The standard libraries are provided in this format in OSF/1.

Note that this scheme still allows symbol substitution—for example, an alternative version of *printf( )* can be substituted at load time for the version in the
shared library using packages (§10.9 - §10.11). Also note that the locations to
which shared routines have been pre-relocated can be changed without the need
for re-linking. This is all possible because final symbol resolution can occur at
load time, as described in the next section.

10.5

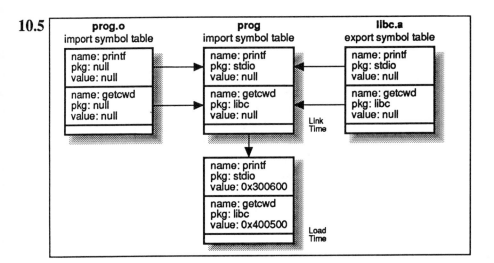

The run-time loader

OSF/1 has redesigned the role of the linker and loader so that their tasks are performed in two stages:

- In the first stage, when the *ld* (or *gld*) program is run on an object module to create an executable file, it no longer copies and resolves external symbols as it comes to their definitions, but maintains a table (called an **import symbol table**) listing the unresolved symbols and the modules in which they can be found. No library modules are actually copied into the executable file. Similarly, when definitions of symbols are found, they are listed in an **export symbol table**.

- When the executable file is run, the linking/loading process is completed. At that time, the loader searches for all unresolved symbols in each import symbol table and extracts their definitions using the export symbol tables of linked modules. In turn, the extracted modules may have their own symbol tables, so those are resolved as well. As symbol resolution is performed, relocation is also performed. The program is then "loaded" into memory and executed.

The result is that when *printf()* is called, all the linker does is make an entry in the import symbol table. When the program is executed, the run-time loader examines the import symbol table, sees that *printf()* is needed, and supplies its reserved address to the executable image. In this way, shared libraries are supported by the OSF/1 loader.

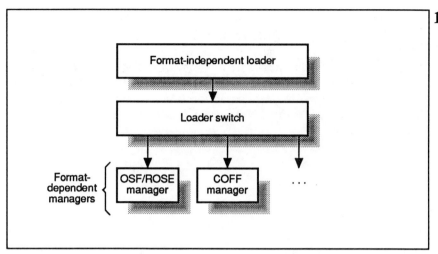

10.6

Multiple format support

An important goal of the OSF/1 loader was to support multiple object file formats. OSF/1 had to make it easy for vendors to use their own proprietary file formats, but also provide support for an OSF-designed object file format. By supporting multiple file formats, the loader is said to be **extensible**.

The OSF-designed object file format is called OSF/ROSE, based on the Mach-O file format developed at Carnegie Mellon University. It was expanded by OSF for extensibility and to support packages (§10.9) and shared libraries (§10.4).

To support multiple file formats, the run-time loader was designed to be broken into two parts: a single **format-independent loader** and multiple **format-dependent managers**. For a file format to be supported, it simply needs its own format-dependent manager written. The format-dependent manager provides routines for creating import and export tables, relocation, dynamic loading and unloading, and other format-specific loader functions. These routines are selected and called through an interface called the **loader switch**.

The loader switch contains an entry for each built-in format-dependent manager. Each entry in turn contains pointers to the format-dependent routines. When a file is executed, the loader asks each of the built-in format-dependent managers whether the file is recognizable to them. Once the format of the executable file is recognized by a manager, all subsequent format-dependent procedures are passed to that manager.

Format-dependent managers can also be added dynamically. If the loader switch exhausts all built-in format-dependent managers, it consults a list of dynamically-loadable format-dependent managers, individually loading them and asking whether they recognize the executable file format. The advantage to this is that the loader can remain small by statically including only the frequently-used for-mat-dependent managers. Another advantage is that testing new format-depen-dent managers is much easier, since adding a new manager does not require rebuilding the loader.

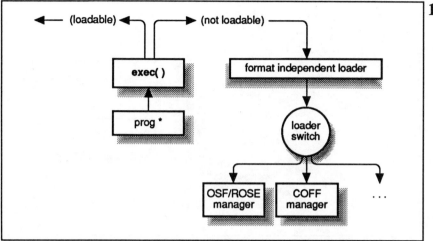

Extensions to exec()

Programs are loaded on UNIX systems through the *exec()* system call. In traditional UNIX systems, any program called by *exec()* must have all external symbols resolved and be fully relocated. As you can imagine, this throws a wrench into the design of the run-time loader and support of shared libraries.

Relocated programs that have no unresolved references can still be run with *exec()* on OSF/1, but *exec()* has been restructured so that any program that cannot be directly loaded is passed to the run-time loader, using the *exec_with_loader()* routine. When a program is executed with *exec()*, the system call handler examines the program and behaves as follows:

- If the program is in a recognizable load format, is fully relocated, and contains no unresolved references, then the program is loaded directly, and control is passed to the program on return to user mode.

- If the program cannot be directly loaded, however, the *exec_with_loader()* function is called, which passes control to the run-time loader along with the name of the program to be loaded. The loader links the program to shared libraries, loads additional modules as required, and relocates the resulting executable in system memory as necessary. Through the loader switch (§10.6), the loader can also support file formats that may not be recognized by *exec()*.

10.8

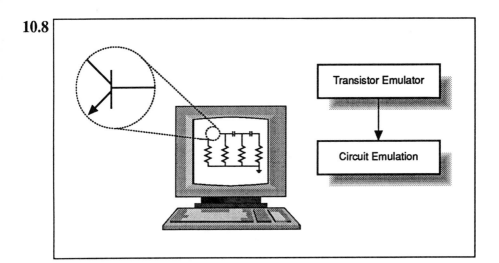

Dynamic loading and unloading

Modules may be explicitly loaded into or unloaded from a running program. For example, in a CAD/CAM application, one might put a transistor into a diagram. A side effect of this decision might be to load a transistor emulation module into the program. If one subsequently decides to remove the transistor from the diagram, then one might want to unload the emulation module as well.

To make this possible, the run-time loader remains in the address space even after the program starts up. A program can call the *load*( ) and *unload*( ) functions to load or unload a module dynamically. By dynamically loading and unloading modules that are not frequently used in the program, a programmer can keep the executable image of the program small.

In addition, modules can be loaded and unloaded from another process, Cross-process loading, however, is only currently supported for dynamically loading and unloading modules in the kernel. Dynamic kernel loading is used in conjunction with dynamic configuration to support loadable and unloadable device drivers (§5.4), streams modules and drivers, file systems, and network protocols. Kernel loading is managed by a privileged user-mode task called the **kernel loader server**. This server maintains the data structures describing the kernel address space (i.e., the same types of data structures that describe a user task).

10.9

Packages are abstractions of libraries

- symbols are associated with packages, not libraries
- packages can be redefined at run time

Packages

The concept of **packages** evolved in OSF/1 to provide more flexibility in symbol resolution and to deal with some of the problems generated by shared libraries.

A package is an abstraction of a library, providing access to libraries without directly binding symbols to the libraries or other object modules they are defined in. Unresolved symbols are assigned a package name in the import symbol table when they are linked (§10.5), but it is not determined which library or object module that package actually corresponds to until the run-time loader is called (§10.5). This allows the programmer to redefine the package at load time without having to relink the file.

Using packages, libraries can be moved by a system administrator without requiring programs to be relinked. Since libraries are not always installed in the same place on all systems, this helps make programs more portable. Also, packages help avoid conflicts between symbols of different libraries—for example, both the System V and BSD versions of the *nice()* function are supported in OSF/1. Without packages, we would have to use explicit library pathnames in the import symbol table to avoid conflicts between the *libc* and *libbsd* versions of *nice()*. With packages, we can bind symbols to a package name but redefine that package later. As long as there aren't any naming conflicts within that package, no confusion can occur.

Each package is contained entirely by one object module, but each object module can contain one or more packages. Packages normally correspond to libraries, but programmers are free to subdivide a library's routines into multiple packages.

10.10

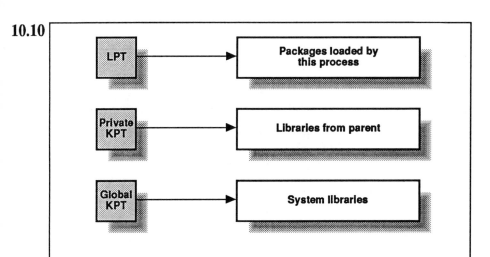

Package tables

In resolving symbols, the loader uses **package tables** to determine which object module or library module contains the definition for that symbol. Package tables contain mappings from package names to library names. A package table is **known** if it is inherited by processes. Associated with each process is a sequence of package tables that is searched to resolve a particular symbol.

The order of search is:

- **Loaded package table**
  A per-process table referring to packages that have been implicitly loaded into the program via an *exec( )* call and those packages that have been explicitly loaded into the program by using the *load( )* function.

- **Private known package table**
  A table maintained by the user and inherited copy-on-write from the parent task.

- **Global known package table**
  A system-wide table maintained by the system administrator used to define the standard system libraries.

The private known package table can be used by the programmer to override the system-wide packages. The loaded package table overrides both the private and global known package tables.

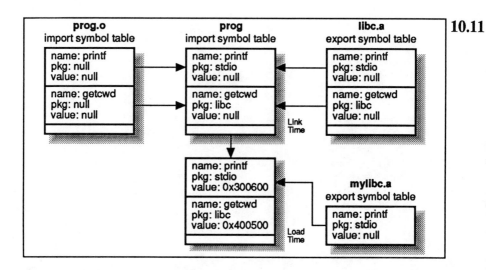

10.11

Using the private package table

Symbol resolution can be changed by using the private package table. In this example, we have defined a private package containing a redefinition of *printf( )*. Note, however, that since the unresolved symbol *printf( )* has already had *stdio* assigned as its package name in the import symbol table, the private package table needs to be assigned the name *stdio* as well in order to override the definition in the global known package table.

Since the private package table is searched before the globally known package table, our version of *printf( )* is the one that is used. However, since our private package only defines *printf( )*, any other symbols paired with the *stdio* package are still satisfied through the *stdio* package on the globally known package table.

11

PROGRAMMING UNDER OSF/1:
Using Threads

IN THIS CHAPTER

- Mach threads and POSIX threads

- Threads offer advantages and challenges

- How to approach a multi-threaded program

- Creating a thread

- How to service a request

- Synchronizing memory accesses with mutual exclusion locks

- Condition variables provide another kind of synchronization

- How to use a condition variable

- Threads easily handle asynchronous events

- Canceling threads

- POSIX threads solve re-entrant problems

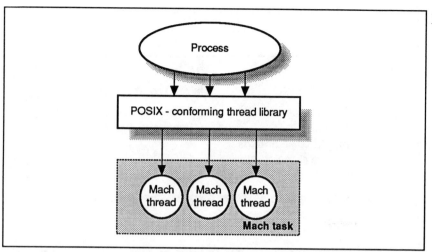

11.1

Mach threads and POSIX threads

A thread is a single, sequential flow of execution—that is, a "lightweight process" executing serially on a single processor, one instruction at a time. UNIX processes can consist of multiple threads, possibly executing simultaneously, or "in parallel".

The application programmer's threads are not Mach threads. The Mach threads we described earlier (§2.1) are the lowest-level implementation of threads. OSF/1, however, presents to the programmer a higher-level thread interface that conforms to the draft POSIX 1003.4a standard. These latter threads—often called POSIX threads, or Pthreads—are implemented using Mach threads. A programming library accepts thread calls in POSIX syntax, and creates Mach threads as necessary, adding the higher-level thread management that Mach does not provide and POSIX requires.

Mach threads remain directly available, however. These give more direct thread control to the programmer, at the price of increased responsibility. For example, when you issue a Mach thread-creation call, the newly created thread has no program counter or stack pointer. You must create a stack yourself, call a thread-set-state routine to set the registers, and finally issue a thread-resume call to actually start the thread. All this is machine-dependent, and is not the way most applications will choose to go.

In the rest of this chapter, "threads" means POSIX threads, unless we explicitly refer to "Mach threads". Note that the draft POSIX 1003.4a standard is expected to become final in 1991.

11.2

Why use threads?	Thread requirements:
• Performance gain	• Managing shared memory
• Portability	• Synchronizing on events
• Simplified algorithms	
• They're cheap	

Threads offer advantages and challenges

The greatest motivation for using threads lies in the potential for **performance gain**. Threads let you use all CPUs on a multiprocessor machine. Even on a uniprocessor machine threads can offer certain performance benefits. For example, they allow you to overlap (in a timesharing manner) I/O activity and computation. That is, the threads of a task are independently scheduled for execution on the processor, and if a thread performing I/O should block, the other threads can continue making use of their allotted slices of processor time.

Threads enable you to parallelize your program without sacrificing **portability**. Using threads, you can develop an application in a uniprocessor environment and know that it will run on any multiprocessor machine implementing POSIX threads. And likewise you can write a program taking advantage of a truly parallelized environment, knowing that it will still run if transported to a non-parallelized machine that supports POSIX threads.

Many problems yield most naturally to a solution involving threads. When a programming task decomposes into several relatively independent strands, the non-threaded version is typically tangled, requiring complicated bookkeeping on the current state of many different activities. A program like that often evolves into something like a mini-scheduler. In contrast, a multi-threaded program takes advantage of the scheduling and resource management offered by the operating system. Unlike the non-threaded program, if one part of its activity needs to be suspended for some period, the other threads can continue execution.

Note that threads give you the advantages of parallelism without consuming many resources. Since the operating system can create threads easily, it is reasonable to use many of them in a single program, if the program can make good use of them.

The challenges posed by threads relate mostly to the fact that threads share nearly all the resources of their parent process, and therefore can get in the way of each other. There are two ways in which they typically must find a means of coordination:

One has to do with **mutual access to shared memory resources**. Imagine what would happen if two threads attempted to update a linked list at the same time. There needs to be a way for each thread to know when the list is free, and when it is being modified by the other process. Threads can use locks for this purpose (§11.6).

Similarly, threads must sometimes **synchronize themselves with particular events**. They can achieve this with signaling mechanisms (§11.7).

11.3

Multi-threaded server example
- Simple main program
- Each thread handles one request
- Individual threads can block

How to approach a multi-threaded program

Let's take a look at an application using multiple threads in a server. We'll assume the server is an appointment manager and waits for service requests on many channels simultaneously. It maintains a database in main memory.

Since the database is held in process memory, the separate threads can easily share access to it. Each thread waits for input on a separate input channel and then handles the service request. If one thread blocks while processing a request, the other threads continue executing. Another common design requires only a single thread to wait for service requests and then create a separate thread to handle each one.

Why can't this same approach employ separate processes? Actually, it can. For example, the common telnet daemon spawns separate processes to handle requests to log in to remote machines. This is made easier because the processes do not need to share memory. However, performance can still suffer due to the relatively heavy overhead in creating processes.

The advantages of threads for our application, then, are these:

- a very simple main program receives requests and assigns each to a thread

- we gain program modularity and a simplified overall program design by virtue of the fact that service requests map to threads one-on-one—there is no multiplexing code

- there is parallelism, with requests serviced simultaneously on multiple processors. Even in a single-CPU system, I/O and computation can be concurrent

11.4

```
void doarequest () ;

do while (1) {
/* Wait for new request */
  . . .
/* Create and start thread to handle the request */
ret = pthread_create (&newthread,
      pthread_attr_default, doarequest, channel) ;
}
```

Creating a thread

The top-level code of our appointment manager executes an endless loop waiting for requests (on some unspecified communication channel) to store or retrieve data. Upon receiving such a request, the code invokes **pthread_create** to create a new thread that will service the request. The call takes these arguments:

- the address of an integer variable in which the operating system can place an identifier for the new thread (**&newthread**)

- an argument specifying various attributes of the new thread. In this example the default attributes are requested by **pthread_attr_default**.

- the address of the function the new thread should begin executing (**doarequest**)

- a scalar value (**channel** in this example) to be passed to the specified function

When the **pthread_create** call returns successfully, the new thread has begun execution. (Note that we omit all error checking from the code fragments for simplicity's sake.) The main program loop does not need to bother with its off-spring further; the thread will terminate by calling **pthread_exit** when it finishes its work.

11.5

```
doarequest (channel)
. . .
{
    operation = readchan (channel);
    key = readchan (channel);
    /* lock the database here - see the next example */
    switch (operation) {
        get: writechan (channel, database [key]);
        set: database [key] = readchan (channel);
    }
    /* unlock the database here */
}
```

How to service a request

The new thread is now executing **doarequest**. It expects to receive through its communication channel two pieces of data: the designation of an operation to perform, and a key specifying which record of the database to perform the operation on. The operation can be either to 1) read the indicated record of the database and write it to the communications channel; or 2) read the communications channel and write the received message into the record of the database.

However, if our appointment manager is servicing several requests, these threads may be running concurrently. Therefore, we cannot assume undisturbed access to the database. That is why the code shows the database being locked (by an as yet unspecified method) immediately before it is accessed, and unlocked immediately afterwards.

11.6

```
doarequest (channel)
...
{
    operation = readchan (channel);
    key = readchan (channel);
    pthread_mutex_lock (db_mutex);
    switch (operation) {
        get: writechan (channel, database [key]);
        set: database [key] = readchan (channel);
    }
    pthread_mutex_unlock (db_mutex);
}
```

Synchronizing memory accesses with mutual exclusion locks

A **mutual exclusion lock** (sometimes called a "mutex") is simply a piece of memory—identified by some element of a data structure—which one thread has established as a lock by calling the **pthread_mutex_init** library routine (not shown in this example). This is typically done at thread initialization. Thereafter, other threads can set the lock by passing the address of the memory location to **pthread_mutex_lock**.

But while all threads will now have access to the same lock, it is the nature of these locks to allow only one thread to apply the lock at any given time. If thread A has applied the lock and thread B then attempts to apply the same lock, B will block, waiting until the lock is free. Mutual exclusion locks enable threads to coordinate their actions upon specific resources, effectively serializing access to shared data.

However, the example as shown has limitations. The lock prevents simultaneous access, not only to the particular part of the database a thread is currently reading or writing, but to the database as a whole. This prevents simultaneous access even when there is no threat of conflict. The solution is to allocate more than one lock at thread-initialization time, one lock for each of multiple segments of the database. If the threads obtained one lock for each individual record, then the two locking calls shown above could be:

```
pthread_mutex_lock(db_mutex[key]);
...
pthread_mutex_unlock(db_mutex[key]);
```

11.7

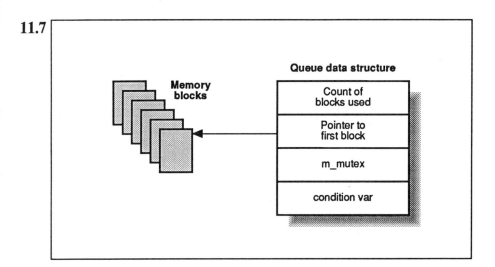

Condition variables provide another kind of synchronization

Threads commonly must wait for some condition to become true. Suppose, for example, that an application must deal with a group of memory blocks, and views these blocks as some sort of queue. The blocks, managed by means of a queue data structure, are linked together; when the last block has been allocated, the next thread needing a block must wait until one is freed.

Suppose further that, to protect both the queue data structure and the memory blocks themselves, mutual exclusion locks are used. To obtain an empty block, a thread places a lock on the data structure (the piece of memory used for the lock is actually part of the data structure). Then it modifies the structure by decrementing the block count, and removes the lock. Similarly, a thread desiring to free a memory block places a lock on the queue structure, increments the count, and removes the lock.

The problem here is that, when all memory blocks have been allocated and a thread places a lock on the queue in order to obtain a new lock, it will have to wait until one is freed. But how will any other process free a block so long as the first process holds the lock?

To avoid this problem, the threads should use a **condition variable**, allowing any thread to wait until some condition is true—in this case, until a block of memory is freed. Upon finding all memory blocks used, a thread immediately releases its lock and begins to wait on the condition.

11.8

```
acquire_resource (resource)
...
{
    ret = pthread_mutex_lock (resource_lock);
    while (resource.count==0) {
        ret = pthread_cond_wait (resource.cond, resource.lock);
    }

    my_resource = dequeue (resource.queue);
    resource.count--;
    ret = pthread_mutex_unlock (mutex);
    return (my_resource);
}
```

How to use a condition variable

The call to **pthread_cond_wait** accomplishes both the release of the lock (§11.7) and the conditional wait in a single stroke. The thread is suspended until another thread issues a matching **pthread_cond_signal** call. More specifically, these two actions are performed by **pthread_cond_wait**:

- it releases the lock passed to it as its second argument. (The call will fail if the lock was already released.)
- it waits on the condition passed as its first argument

A thread thus suspended will resume execution only when another thread frees a memory block and signals that the condition causing the wait is no longer in effect. That can happen like this:

```
release_resource(resource)
....
{
    ret = pthread_mutex_lock(m_mutex);
    enqueue(resource.queue, resource);
    resource.count++;
    ret = pthread_mutex_unlock(m_mutex);
    ret = pthread_cond_signal(resource.cond);
}
```

On returning a memory block to the pool, a thread locks the queue data structure, increments the block count, unlocks the queue, and signals any thread that may be waiting for free memory blocks. A related routine, **pthread_cond_broadcast**, may be used to signal multiple threads waiting on the same condition.

11.9

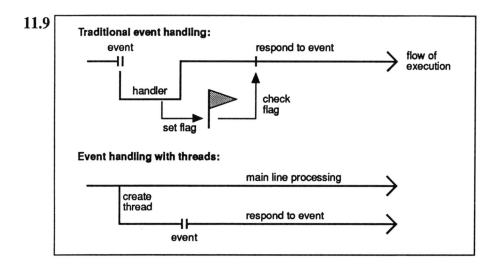

Threads easily handle asynchronous events

Our earlier example illustrates how threads can respond to a certain kind of asynchronous event. Here we offer some brief comments upon the more general issue of asynchronicity.

Many applications must handle asynchronous events—events that occur outside the predetermined flow of program instructions. For example, a timer may expire, or "out of band" information may arrive over a communications line. In such cases, it is required both that the asynchronous event be attended to, and that it not "barge in" upon the application's current activity with disruptive effect.

Asynchronous events are traditionally handled at the "interrupt level"—that is, by a trap or signal handler. Since it is often inconvenient to process an interrupt immediately upon its arrival—there may be other business that needs finishing first—the signal handler sets some sort of a global flag indicating that the signal occurred, and then yields to the previously executing activity. The response to the interrupt must then wait for some regularly scheduled piece of code that is prepared to "notice" the global flag. And even if no wait is really necessary, it may be inconvenient to move the code for responding to the event from the main body of the application to the signal handler.

In a threaded environment, such applications can dedicate a thread to wait for a particular event. The indirection—and delay—associated with signal handlers is thereby avoided. Also, the code is less circuitous, because the recognition of the event and the response to it occur in the same place.

11.10

Two cancelation policies:
- General cancelation (on or off)
- Asynchronous cancelation (on or off)

Cleanup routines:
- Specified by threads themselves
- Execute upon cancelation

Canceling threads

It may be desirable, in the normal course of an application, for one thread to cancel another. For example, a chess program may start up several threads to examine different attack strategies. If one thread should happen to discover a forced win, it might reasonably cancel all the others.

But even conceding the value of such life-and-death powers, questions of timing remain. If a sentenced thread happens to be updating a data structure such as a linked list, then a reprieve—however short—is probably advisable for the good of the larger society. After all, at least one thread—the executioner—will continue running, and may need access to that linked list. So there are times when it is safe to cancel a thread, and times when it isn't; only the victim knows.

Each thread can control two cancelation policies with respect to itself:

General cancelation. If this is disabled, the thread cannot be canceled at all. Otherwise, it can. A cancelation decree directed at the thread while general cancelation is disabled is queued pending a change in the policy. The default policy is "disabled".

Asynchronous cancelation. A disabled asynchronous cancelation policy means that the thread cannot be canceled arbitrarily; it will yield up the ghost at specified cancelation points only. The enabled policy, on the other hand, allows cancelation at any time—a policy that is suitable only for threads lacking all power to screw things up from beyond the grave. By default, asynchronous cancelation is disabled.

Each thread possesses a stack for **cleanup routines**. The thread can push routines onto the stack and pop them off. These routines get called immediately before a canceled thread expires. As they run, asynchronous cancelation is disabled—there's no use shooting a man who is already hanging from a rope.

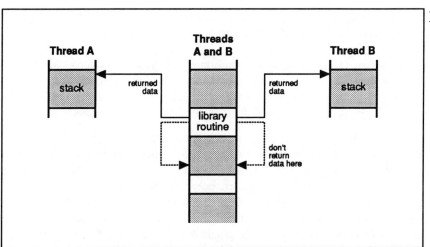

11.11

POSIX threads solve re-entrant problems

The use of threads forces those who design programming environments to solve the problem of re-entrancy. This problem—common, but not always highly visible, on UNIX systems—arises when a library routine currently in use by one part of an application is executed ("re-entered") by another part of the application, so that two or more instances of the same routine are executing at the same time in the address space of a single process.

This can happen on UNIX systems, for example, whenever a signal handler calls a non-re-entrant routine such as *fwrite(3)*—or any other buffered I/O routine—which the interrupted code may also be calling.

Suppose that two threads of a single process are simultaneously running the same library routine. These threads, you will recall, share the same address space—although each has been given its own stack. Here, then, are two ways the re-entrant problem can occur:

- The library routine might use memory structures other than the stack for returning data to the calling threads. (Variables declared **static** in C are an example of such structures.) In this case, the data returned to the second thread will overwrite the data returned to the first thread. For the library routine—with all its static data structures—resides at a fixed location in the memory space of the process, which is the same memory space for each of the threads.

- The library routine might also save state data in static memory structures between calls. For example, it might need to know how many times it has been invoked. But it needs this information relative to a single thread; therefore, invocations by a different thread will render the data inaccurate.

OSF/1 solves these problems by conforming to POSIX standards. Most library routines have been re-written for re-entrancy—or, if that cannot be done because of the semantics of a routine, a separate, re-entrant version of the routine is provided. (These routines usually have an appended "_r" in their names.)

All this complicates the programming environment, however. The POSIX 1003.4a standard labels certain re-entrant capabilities "optional". This means that a POSIX threads implementation could omit them while remaining compliant with the standard. To allow programmers to write code portable across all 1003.4a implementations while still taking advantage of the optional features, it was necessary to specify certain compile-time symbols that programmers can use to test for feature availability. The program must then have a work-around if, for example, a re-entrant call is not available.

12

PROGRAMMING UNDER OSF/1:

Internationalization

IN THIS CHAPTER

- Internationalization and localization

- ISO character sets

- Data transparency

- Japanese characters

- Wide and multi-byte characters

- Collation issues

- Character and equivalence classes

- Date and time specifications in different cultures

- Locales combine language, territory, and codeset

- LANG and LC_* environment variables define a locale

- setlocale( ) sets the run-time locale for a program

- nl_langinfo( ) assigns locale information

- Message catalogs provide messages in multiple languages

12.1

> **Localization** is converting a program for use in another locale.
>
> **Internationalization** is converting a program to be independent of its current locale.

Internationalization and localization

Imagine using an application that was written for another language. Forget about the obscure names of the commands and their options—you suspect that some of them, like "grep", don't make that much sense for most Americans, either! But imagine that the program ends prematurely, and the error message is in a different language. Or that it prompts for a "y" or "n" answer, and you want to answer, "oui". Or imagine that you enter a date as August 3rd and it is read as March 8th.

For many years, the only solution to this problem was for non-English-speaking vendors of UNIX to alter the application directly, similar to the way you would translate a book from English to Russian. As you can imagine, this became exceedingly inefficient, not to mention frustrating to non-English speakers.

To support multiple languages and cultures, it became critical for operating systems to be **internationalized**. An internationalized program can be run in different languages or "locales" without itself being changed.

Although language is clearly the dominating factor in internationalization, there are many other factors that need to be taken into account. The word **locale** is used to specify all facets of a particular culture. **Localization** is the process of converting a program into a form appropriate for a given locale.*

---

* Internationalization is sometimes abbreviated to I18N (the letter "i" followed by 18 letters followed by the letter "n"). Similarly, localization is abbreviated to L10N.

In the past, localization was the painstaking process of translating the entire program into a new language. Multiple copies of the same program resulted, one for each translation—so a single bug fix would have to be duplicated multiple times.

If a program has been internationalized, however, all locale-specific information can be supplied at run time, and localization can be completed by simply providing the information corresponding to that locale. The programs themselves can remain untouched, so only one version need be maintained.

For a simple example, if a program has it built in to accept a "yes" or "no" answer, the program needs to be adjusted explicitly to accept "oui" or "non" in order to run in French. However, if instead of accepting only "yes" or "no" explicitly, the program looks for a response matching either the YESSTR or NOSTR environment variable (which can be set by the locale), localization no longer requires changing the program itself. You need only set things up so that the YESSTR and NOSTR environment variables are assigned properly for users. This is clearly an easier way to go about things.

OSF/1 concentrates on internationalizing programs, not on localizing them—that is, OSF/1 simply provides the flexibility for vendors to add functionality for new locales, but does not supply full support for any locales except American English.*

Since not all readers may be familiar with some of the broader issues for internationalization, this chapter gives an overview of some of the more significant internationalization problems, with emphasis on the OSF solutions only towards the end of the chapter.

---

* Although locale information is provided for other locales (§12.10), OSF/1 supplies message catalogs (§12.13) only for American English.

12.2

Formal name	Informal name	Languages covered
ISO 8859/1	Latin-1	Western European
ISO 8859/2	Latin-2	Eastern European
ISO 8859/3	Latin-3	Southeastern European
ISO 8859/4	Latin-4	Northern European
ISO 8859/5	Latin-5	English & Cyrillic-Based
ISO 8859/6	Latin-6	English & Arabic
ISO 8859/7	Latin-7	English & Greek
ISO 8859/8	Latin-8	English & Hebrew
ISO 8859/9	Latin-9	Western European & Turkish

ISO character sets

Things were really convenient for American programmers when the ASCII character set could always be relied on. If you wanted to alphabetize a list, you could just compare integer values, since 'B' was guaranteed to come right after 'A'. If you wanted to turn a lowercase letter into an uppercase letter or vice-versa, you could just toggle the 6th bit or add/subtract ('a' - 'A'). And then there was the convenience of there being only 128 characters represented by ASCII, so you also had a whole bit left over in each character byte to play with. The 8th bit could be used to mark characters in special ways, a great shortcut for many applications.

The result was that a lot of code took advantage of the ASCII character set, and consequently a lot of code now needs to be rewritten for internationalization.

The familiar ASCII character set includes 'a-z', 'A-Z', '0-9', punctuation marks, a bunch of control characters, and other special characters to boot. But it's inadequate for any language but English. To compensate for ASCII's shortcomings, the International Standards Organization (ISO) extended ASCII by using the 8th bit and defining values 128-255. These values are used for alphabetic characters that aren't used in English—for example, 'æ', 'ø', and 'å' are Dutch characters with no English equivalents.

There are actually several different ISO character sets, combining ASCII English with Western European languages, with Eastern European languages, with Arabic or Greek, etc. The ISO character set that incorporates Western European characters is officially called ISO 8859/1, but it is usually referred to as Latin-1.

12.3

> Support for ISO character sets in OSF/1
> requires **data transparency**.
> - Programs are 8 bit clean
> - File names are not truncated
> - *tty* driver avoids masking with octal 177

Data transparency

The most immediate complication that the ISO character sets produce is that the 8th bit of a character byte is no longer up for grabs. If programs need to be compatible with other locales, they need to use all 8 bits of a byte for input and output. This is called being **8-bit clean**, or **data transparent**.

All of OSF/1 is guaranteed to be data transparent. For example, the *tty* driver treats all characters as 8-bit, not 7-bit ASCII, and avoids masking with octal 177. In addition, traditional UNIX commands that use the sign bit to encode extra information (for example *vi* and *nroff*) have been re-written.

So support of the ISO character set, which extends ASCII to include European languages, largely involves cleaning up code that previously ignored or reassigned the 8th bit of a character byte. But European languages are not the end of the story. The second largest UNIX market in the world, after the United States, is Japan.

12.4

> **Kanji** is the Japanese ideographic language, with thousands of characters.
>
> **Katakana** is the Japanese phonetic language used for foreign words.
>
> Two encoding schemes are widely used for Japanese characters: SJIS and EUC/UJIS

Japanese characters

Japanese (and other ideographic languages) provides a whole new set of compli-cations for character representation. There are three written languages in Japan: **Hiragana, Katakana,** and **Kanji.** Hiragana and Katakana are both phonetic (**Kana**) languages, while Kanji is the ideographic "official" language of Japan.

There are several thousand Kanji characters, but only somewhere around 48 char-acters in each Kana language. Katakana is the language designed for foreign words, and for that reason, keyboards in Japan generally use Katakana symbols. However, when symbols are typed, they are often translated directly into the Kanji character matching the phonetic pronunciation.

For encoding Japanese characters, the Japanese Institute of Standards (JIS) came up with a multi-byte code set (§12.5), which has been incorporated into other code sets. There are two major character encoding schemes that use JIS: Shift-JIS and EUC/UJIS.

Shift-JIS (also known as SJIS) is commonly used by both mainframe computers and PCs in Japan, and is so-called because the internal encoding of JIS has been shifted "up" out of the way of ASCII encoding, permitting both ASCII and JIS characters to be intermixed. Shift-JIS characters may be either one byte (7-bit ASCII or Katakana) or two bytes (Kanji and miscellaneous).

EUC/UJIS incorporates characters for other ideographic Asian languages (such as Chinese and Korean). OSF/1 currently supports Shift-JIS, and 1.1 will extend the environment to include EUC/UJIS as another distinct locale.

12.5

- **Wide characters (wchar_ts)** are implementation–defined: they are a fixed size, as large as necessary for the character set.
- **Multi-byte characters** can be different sizes within the same data stream.

The kernel, tty driver and system libraries in OSF/1 have been adapted to support multi-byte and wide characters.

Wide and multi-byte characters

Obviously, the old assumption that one-character-equals-one-byte is no longer reliable. ANSI C recognized the difficulty by defining the typedef **wchar_t** to be as wide as necessary to hold the largest character in your code set.

Although wide characters (**wchar_ts**) can be defined to whatever size you like with a **typedef** statement, they are guaranteed to be the same size throughout a program. **Multi-byte characters**, on the other hand, differ from wide characters in that the characters in a single data stream can be different sizes. The EUC and SJIS encoding methods (§12.4) are both examples of multi-byte code sets because they combine single-byte ASCII with double-byte or quadruple-byte ideographic character encodings.

In general, data is encoded in wide character format for internal processing, because it is usually easier to process data if it is all the same size. However, data is usually stored to disk in multi-byte format to save space where we can—so Kanji characters can be stored with as many as four bytes, but ASCII characters can be stored with only one. Wide and multi-byte characters are supported in OSF/1 in the following ways:

- In the kernel, the *tty* driver can process backspace properly in order to back up over a multi-byte character. (The kernel also guarantees that a multi-byte character in a filename will never be truncated, since the kernel never truncates filenames.)
- In the system libraries, there is full support for wide-character and wide-string processing. In addition, the **curses** library has been adapted to handle multi-byte characters.

12.6

> • Collation in English depends heavily on ASCII sequencing.
>
> • Other languages can not rely on their code set for collation.

Collation issues

As you can see, there's enough to worry about in just determining how to represent the characters for other languages. We haven't even begun on the problems that the languages themselves present.

Collation presents some of the most difficult problems in internationalization. Next time you run the *ls* command, take a look at the sequence of the files printed. If you had a choice, you might want files listed in another sequence—for example, with uppercase and lowercase characters intermixed—but all in all, the *ls* command lists things in a nice sequence. We depend on the *ls* command for giving us a listing of our files in alphabetical order.

Most people know that the *ls* command simply lists things using ASCII sequencing. Well, this is convenient for English speakers, but isn't really tailor-made for other languages. Other languages have their own ideas of how words should be sorted. The *ls* command isn't a big deal—after all, it's just a listing of files, and having it in order just makes it easier to find things—but the *sort* command is another story. By definition, users expect *sort* to produce a "correct" order. This is a bit more difficult if you can't rely on your character code set having the letters of your alphabet in the right order. This is even more difficult if your language doesn't use an alphabet!

UNIX collation algorithms are appropriate (mostly) for English, but not for the rest of the world. We assume that if we want to know if a word comes before another in a sorted sequence, it's just a matter of comparing the first character of *String1* against the first character of *String2*; if it's a tie, then we compare the second character of *String1* against the second character of *String2*; and so on. Consider now the following complications in European languages:

- In German, the letter ß needs to be sorted as if it were "ss".

- In Spanish, "ch" and "ll" are treated as separate letters. That is, the Spanish dictionary is in the order "A", "B", "C", "Ch", "D", etc.—so all words beginning with "ch" are actually sorted after all other words beginning with "c", and all words beginning with "ll" are sorted after all other words beginning with "l".

- In French, the letters 'a', 'á', 'à', and 'â' are all considered equivalent in primary collation order, and use a secondary collation order only in case of a tie (similar to the way upper and lower case letters are intermixed in a dictionary).

These problems are addressed in OSF/1 using equivalence classes and character classes (§12.7). However, the complications that Asian languages present are not as simple:

- In Thai, an alphabetic language is used, but words aren't sorted according to the first character. Instead, they are sorted according to the first vowel in the word.

- Ideographic languages like Japanese, Chinese and Korean don't use an alphabet, but instead use collections of symbols. In Japanese, the most convenient way to sort words is by their Kana phonetic pronunciation (§12.4), but if they are written in Kanji, then two sequential characters might have no clear connection in their written form. Their sorting information therefore cannot be deciphered from the written character alone.

OSF/1 does not currently support sorting by first vowel or by ideographic characters.

12.7

> Character classes are in the form [:*class*:]
>   Where *class* is one of:
>   alpha, upper, lower, digit, xdigit,
>   alnum, space, punct, print, graph,
>   cntrl
>   Equivalence classes are in the form [=*c*=]

Character and equivalence classes

Among everything else that is dependent on ASCII is the syntax for regular expressions. For example, to match any lowercase alphabetic character, one would use a regular expression of the form:

```
[a-z]
```

which is tied to the knowledge that all lowercase alphabetic characters are bounded by the range. (ASCII 97 is 'a', ASCII 98 is 'b', and so on until you reach ASCII 122 = 'z'.) This doesn't work in all languages—for example, in Norwegian, there are alphabetic characters after 'z'.

Improvements to the specification of regular expressions come from the XPG3 standard, in which [a-z] can be expressed as:

```
[[:lower:]]
```

The above expression is an example of a **character classification**. The locale database contains character classification information identifying lowercase alphabetic characters in the current locale. Among the other character classifications are [:upper:] for upper-case characters, [:digit:] for decimal digits, and [:alnum:] for alphanumeric characters.

Equivalence classes can also be used in regular expressions. Equivalence classes are groups of letters that can be considered "equivalent". For example, in French the letters 'a', 'á', 'à', and 'â' are considered equivalent for "primary" sorting purposes. Equivalence classes are specified as [=c=], where c is any of the characters in the group. So the regular expression:

    [[=a=]]

in French is the same as:

    [aáàâ]

12.8

Other cultural differences:

Date notation	. . . 4/20/91 vs. 20-4-91
Time notation	. . . 4:30 vs. 16:30
Monetary notation	. . . $ vs. ¥
Numerical punctuation	. . . 1,234.56 vs. 1.234,56
Names of months	. . . January vs. Enero
Names of days	. . . Sunday vs. Dimanche

Date and time specifications in different cultures

Language is not the only concern for internationalization efforts. Before we get deeper into the implementation of internationalization in OSF/1, let's talk about some of the other issues, such as dates and dollars.

Most Americans put the month before the date, but hardly anyone else does that. The Fourth of July, 1991 appears in the United States as 7/4/91, but it appears in Italian as 4-VII-91 and in French as 4.7.91. In Japanese, it might appear as 3/7/4. (The Japanese often display years as the number of years in the current era, i.e., since the current Emperor has been on the throne.)

Americans also use 12-hour clocks, which others might do in conversation, but hardly ever in written text. So 6:30PM to an American might read 18:30 in England, 18.30 in Germany, or 18h30 in France.

As for numbers—well, beyond the krona-instead-of-dollars issue, many Europeans would have a fit with American numbers. We use a period (.) as a decimal point and a comma (,) as a thousands separator, and many Europeans do it in reverse—so 5,280.33 would read 5.280,33.

Other things to deal with include day of week, month of year, number of hours in a day, etc. There are also cultures that don't have 7-day weeks or 12-month years or 24-hour days—but, luckily, they don't buy that many UNIX systems.

12.9

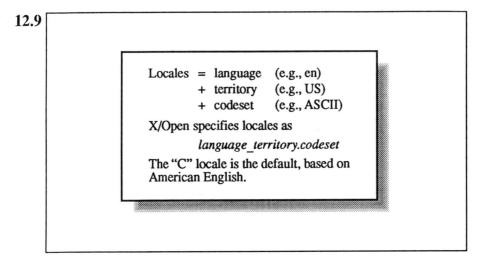

Locales = language   (e.g., en)
        + territory   (e.g., US)
        + codeset   (e.g., ASCII)

X/Open specifies locales as

language_territory.codeset

The "C" locale is the default, based on American English.

Locales combine language, territory, and codeset

Locales clearly aren't just a matter of language. There are generally three parts to a locale: language, territory, and codeset. Unfortunately, there are no rules as yet on how locales should be named.

The "C" locale is defined by ANSI C, and is specified to be the behavior of an American-based system. The POSIX committee specifies a locale named "POSIX", which is pretty much the same as the "C" locale, although there is no guarantee that the two won't diverge. Other than "C" and "POSIX", however, there are currently no guidelines for how locales should be named.

OSF/1 has followed the suggestion of the X/Open committee, which is to represent a locale name with the convention *ll_TT.codeset*. In this scheme, the locale used in the United States can be represented en_US.ASCII. A 2-character code for the language comes first, followed by a 2-character code for the territory, followed by the name of the codeset in 14 bytes or less.

	12.10

Environment variables:

LANG	Language
LC_COLLATE	Collation sequence
LC_CTYPE	ctype information
LC_MONETARY	Monetary notation
LC_NUMERIC	Numeric notation
LC_TIME	Time/Date preferences
LC_MESSAGES	Message catalogs

LANG and LC_* environment variables define a locale

Locales can be set by the system administrator or by the individual user. Some OSF/1 vendors may allow the user to override the default locale set by the system administrator.

Locales are designated by several environment variables. The primary environment variable is LANG, which covers all pieces of the locale. For example, to switch to French, you might enter on the command line:

```
% setenv LANG fr_FR.88591
```

(88591 is the code for Latin-1.) Sometimes, however, you might not want the entire package of your locale—for example, if you are working in English but the names you need to sort are Dutch. For that reason, POSIX requires other environment variables to govern discrete parts of the current locale. Each of these can be set to the name of a different locale.

LANG	The primary environment variable.
LC_COLLATE	The collating sequence for the character set.
LC_CTYPE	Provides information for the C language *ctype* functions (*isalpha( )*, *isupper( )*, etc.)
LC_MONETARY	Designates the currency symbol for that locale.
LC_NUMERIC	Specifies how numbers are formatted.
LC_TIME	Specifies format for date and time.
LC_MESSAGES	Defines strings for "yes" and "no", and the language in which program messages should be displayed.

If any of the LC_* variables are not set, the locale specified by LANG is used. If LANG is not set, the "C" locale is the default.

One problem with providing this sort of flexibility is that there's nothing stopping you from making a mistake. If you were to set LANG to German and LC_COL-LATE to Japanese, you'd probably end up confused, and it might be difficult to find out where the problem is. Another problem is that there's no way to associate a file with the locale it was created in, so if it were read in a different locale later on, problems might easily occur.

OSF/1 supplies locale databases for Belgium, Canada, Denmark, Finland, France, Germany, Italy, Japan, the Netherlands, Norway, Portugal, Spain, Sweden, Switzerland, the United Kingdom, and the United States. Since some of these countries have more than one language, there are actually 19 different locale databases included.

12.11

> **char * setlocale (int** *category,* **const char ****locale***);**
> Where:
> >   *category*   . . . is one of the LC_ environment
> >   variables or LC_ALL
> >
> >   *locale*   . . . is a locale name

setlocale( ) sets the run-time locale for a program

The *setlocale( )* function, originally defined by POSIX, is used to set locales from within a program. The syntax is:

```
setlocale(category, locale);
```

where *category* is one of the LC* environment variables (§12.10) listed previously, and *locale* is a locale name (§12.9). Note that the LANG environment variable cannot be supplied as an argument to *setlocale( )*, but the LC_ALL category can be used in its stead. Programmers should use LC_ALL unless they have a good reason not to, and always specify a null locale name if the program is to be internationalized. (With a null locale name, *setlocale( )* uses the current value of the corresponding environment variable, which is (usually) what you want. If you specify a non-null locale name with *setlocale( )*, you're essentially hard-coding your application to run properly in only that locale!)

It's a good practice to make *setlocale( )* one of the first calls in any internationalized programs, since you never know where locale-specific information might crop up. So a typical use of *setlocale( )* might read:

```
#include <locale.h>
main() {
    setlocale(LC_ALL, "");
    ...
```

Without a call to *setlocale( )*, the "C" locale is used for all locale-specific information.

12.12

---

char * nl_langinfo (nl_item *item*);

Where:

    item ... is a constant defined in **<langinfo.h>**

nl_langinfo( ) will be replaced with **localedef** (POSIX.2)

---

nl_langinfo( ) assigns locale information

We have an idea by now of what sort of information needs to be associated with each locale, and how to retrieve it from within an application. The conspicuous omission is how information actually gets supplied.

POSIX 1003.2 specifies a *localedef* utility for converting source definitions for locales into binaries usable by commands and functions. But 1003.2 is still in draft form, so it could change any day. Instead of waiting for *localedef* to get defined, OSF/1 has adopted the XPG3 method in the interim. In this scheme, the **<langinfo.h>** header file defines constants for holding information for date, time, numeric, etc., and the *nl_langinfo( )* function can be used to point programs to the current value of a given constant. OSF/1 plans to move towards *localedef* once it is fully defined.

In addition, OSF/1 has inherited a *ctab* utility from AIX, which compiles collation and *ctype* information into binary objects.

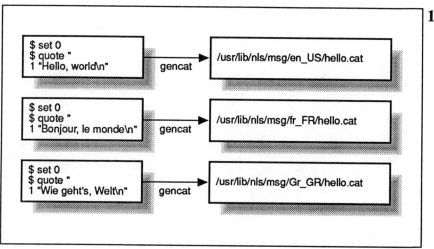

12.13

Message catalogs provide messages in multiple languages

Message catalogs are used to separate message text from application source code. What this means is that instead of a program having it hard-coded to print a message, it reads it from a message catalog. The message catalog used is determined by the value of the LANG environment variable.

Most programs in OSF/1 use message catalogs. Conspicuous exceptions are the kernel, which generates its panic messages in English, and the *ftpd* daemon, which sends ASCII text back to indicate certain serious configuration problems.

Only American-English catalogs are provided by OSF/1, but system vendors can provide additional message catalogs. The *gencat* command can be used to process a source file to produce a direct-access catalog of messages.

The NLSPATH environment variable holds the directory used for message catalogs. OSF/1 sets the default value of NLSPATH to */usr/lib/nls/msg/%L/%N*. When used, "%L" is replaced with the current locale, and "%N" is replaced with the name of the name of the current program with a .cat suffix.

13

LOOKING AHEAD:

What is DCE?

IN THIS CHAPTER

- The networking of the world
- Fundamental distributed services of DCE
- Data-sharing services of DCE
- Scales of operation: cells and groups of cells
- DCE is part of the drive toward standardization
- Operating system and network independence
- Remote procedure calls
- Naming service
- Threads in a distributed computing environment
- Security services
- Distributed file system
- Personal computer integration

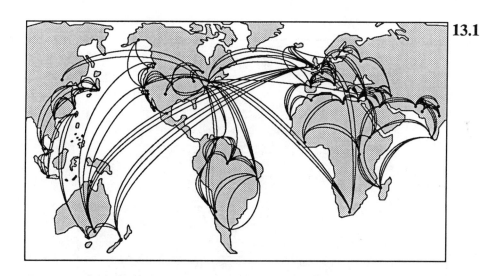

The networking of the world

The world is being networked. Local area nets, already linking personal computers and workstations, are in turn merging into high-speed worldwide networks.

By the end of the decade, wide area nets, T1 connections, fiber optics, and Integrated Services Digital Networks (ISDN) will allow any computer to communicate with millions of other computers as easily as we speak by telephone today.

Computer users require a communications environment, allowing information to flow from wherever it is stored to wherever it is needed. Such an environment must not subject the end user, system manager, or application developer to the extraordinary internal complexities of today's networks.

There is a glaring technological opportunity here. Look at almost any of the innumerable computer installations in the world today, and you will find vast, networked computing resources sitting idle for 75 out of every 100 seconds, while individual users in front of individual machines fret about getting a job done. The resources are there, the technological ability to make use of them is already there, but we haven't yet learned to harness the nearly unlimited computational power latent in the machines all around us.

OSF's Distributed Computing Environment (DCE) is, to date, arguably the most ambitious and large-scale effort to meet this challenge. In this book we seek to acquaint you only with the broad outlines of DCE, largely as those have been sketched by OSF itself. DCE is scheduled for first release in the Fall of 1991.

13.2

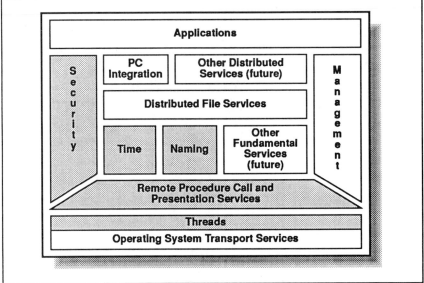

Fundamental distributed services of DCE

The portions of DCE known as "fundamental distributed services" provide tools to software engineers who are creating end-user services. These tools, summarized here, are described more fully in later sections.

Remote procedure call. Known broadly as RPC, this service includes high-level "interface definition languages" together with remote procedure calls. The latter extend the usual notion of a programming language procedure call to embrace interactions between components of distributed systems. Interface definition languages are supported by compilers that convert high-level interface descriptions of remote procedures into C language source code. The resulting procedure calls behave much like local procedure calls.

Sources. Network Computing System (NCS) 2.0, jointly submitted by Digital Equipment Corporation and Hewlett-Packard. This package is an enhanced version of HP-Apollo's NCS.

Naming service. In a distributed environment, information about resources needs to be widely accessible and embodied in meaningful names. The naming (or directory) service allows users and programs to refer conveniently to servers, files, disks, people, and print queues without knowing where they are located in a network. Once obtained, a name remains valid despite many types of network change.

Sources. Distributed Naming Service (DECdns) from Digital Equipment Corporation; and DIR-X X.500 service from Siemens.

Time service. Many distributed applications need to ascertain the order of events, compute the interval between two events, and schedule events independently of where they may occur. A time service makes this possible by synchronizing the clocks in all the component systems of a distributed environment.

Sources. Distributed Time Synchronization Service (DECdts) from Digital Equipment Corporation.

Threads service. Since DCE may be ported to many different operating systems, it does not assume that threads are available as an operating system service. Using re-entrant programming techniques, DCE offers thread facilities that vendors may port to take advantage of native threads. (See §2.1 ff. for discussion of native OSF/1 threads.)

Sources. Concert Multithread Architecture from Digital Equipment Corporation.

Security service. Security concerns multiply in a distributed computing environment. DCE provides facilities for supporting confidentiality in remote procedure calls; a means for authenticating the identity of users and services; management of access permissions; and a registry for user account information.

Sources. Kerberos Version 5 from Project Athena of MIT.

13.3

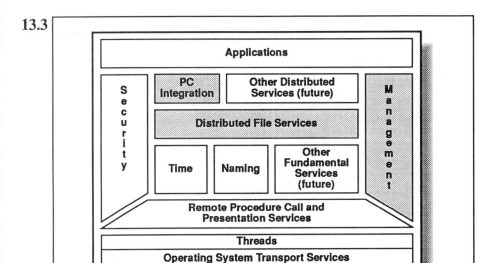

Data-sharing services of DCE

The data-sharing services, summarized briefly here, are described more fully in later sections.

Distributed file system. A distributed computing environment requires not only the ability to make use of CPU cycles throughout a network, but also to store and access data at remote locations. The distributed file system embodies a client/server model that combines local and remote files into a single, expanded file system, with the location of individual files largely transparent to users. Replication of files and directories on multiple machines helps keep applications running when servers fail. Also, there is support for diskless workstations.

Sources. Andrew File System (AFS) 4.0, from Transarc; diskless workstation support (based on AFS) from Hewlett-Packard.

Personal computer integration. While MS-DOS-based personal computers represent a huge installed base, they have rarely been successfully integrated into the larger computing environment. DCE gives PC users access to file and print resources located on hosts implementing DCE. This service depends, however, upon implementation of appropriate clients by the MS-DOS vendors.

Sources. LAN Manager/X from Hewlett-Packard and Microsoft; and (PC)NFS from Sun Microsystems.

System management services. The various management facilities embedded in DCE will, in the future, be integrated into a comprehensive system management architecture by a process similar to the one used in defining DCE. Services are expected to include user/group management, file system management, and license management, among others. See Appendix E on the Distributed Management Environment (DME). The technology selection for the current DME Request for Technology is expected to be made in the Fall of 1991.

13.4

> **Cells**
>
> - arbitrary network scaling
> - simplified, common environments
> - all DCE services available within every cell

Scales of operation: cells and groups of cells

Any given computer in a distributed environment will likely need to communicate more frequently with some computers than others. Managing this complexity becomes more efficient when one applies simplifying common assumptions to the group of machines in frequent communication. This, of course, burdens the less frequently used pathways with greater overhead.

DCE approaches this problem by allowing systems to be grouped into cells. Computers that must communicate often can be placed into a single cell conforming to social, political, or organizational boundaries. Such cells might correspond to a particular local area network, a physical office, or a functional department. Usually, the computers in a cell will be near each other, and used for closely related purposes by people in a single organization. A cell can range in size from two to thousands of computers.

Large systems can be created from multiple cells. A worldwide communications system, for example, might consist of thousands of cells. Computers in such a system will talk to remote cells, though less frequently than they talk to machines in their own cell. Intercell communication typically involves:

- **Longer distances and delays.** The cells may be thousands of miles apart, connected by wide area networks that are slower than local networks.

- **Unknown, probably heterogeneous machines.** Users are likely to make uneducated assumptions about what computers or networks reside in a remote cell.

- **Different administration policies.** Computers in remote cells may be subject to administrative regulations foreign to the local cell.

- **Changing configurations.** Cells may be created changed, moved, or even eliminated between communication sessions.

The cell architecture allows networks to be organized so that these sorts of high-overhead problems occur only with the less-frequent (intercellular) communications. Thus, each cell can be considered a separate management domain for administration and security, making it possible to set up procedures tailored to local conditions, expectations, and needs.

Since every cell must be able to operate independently, it must supply all DCE services for clients within the cell.

13.5

> DCE is an integrated distributed computing environment that promises to become a standard.
>
> DCE also employs many standards. For example:
>
> - TCP/IP
> - UDP
> - DECnet
> - Domain
> - CCITT X.500
> - X/Open (PC connectivity)

DCE is part of the drive toward standardization

Most features of DCE are derived from existing software packages. The added value provided by OSF therefore resides primarily in the integration of these packages into a single environment—an environment that promises to become a "standard" just so far as DCE is adopted by the major operating system vendors (§13.6).

Integration spells interdependence. For example, remote procedure calls use threads, and threads use remote procedure calls. Most of the other DCE components rely on both RPC and threads. Similarly, the security service is thoroughly integrated with the naming service, and the distributed file system draws on all the fundamental services.

Besides the possibility that DCE will become an integrated, overall standard, there is the question of standardization *within* DCE. The numerous internal interfaces present many opportunities to employ recognized standards, and OSF has made a strong effort to do so. These standards range from the TCP, UDP, DECnet, and Domain transport protocols to the CCITT X.500 directory protocols, to the X/Open guidelines for PC connectivity.

In the following sections about particular DCE services, we mention many of the applicable standards.

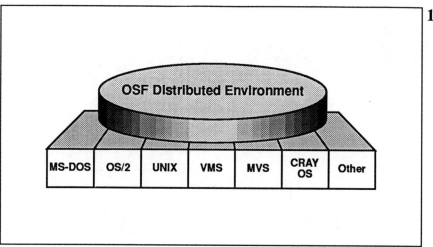

13.6

Operating system and network independence

Written in standard C, DCE makes use of standard interfaces for operating system services, such as POSIX and the various X/Open guidelines.

There are efforts, completed or currently underway, to port DCE to the following operating systems among others: OSF/1, SunOS, AIX, ULTRIX, HP-UX, System V Release 4, VMS, OS/2, CRAY OS, and MVS. The presence of DCE in two different operating systems means that when machines running either operating system are connected to the same network, all the DCE services (§13.2 and §13.3) should work transparently across those machines.

In the next few sections, we'll take a somewhat more detailed look at several of the major building blocks of DCE.

13.7

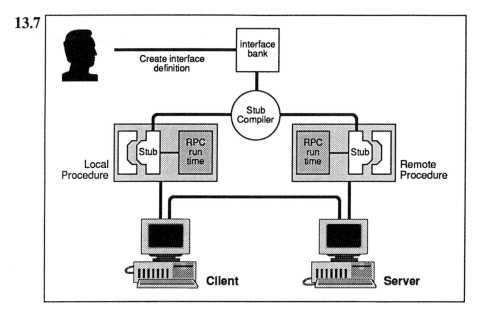

Remote procedure calls

A remote procedure call (RPC) extends the notion of a procedure call to a distributed environment. To the usual mechanics of "executing a procedure" locally, it adds distributed capabilities such as selection of servers and appropriate recovery from communication or server failures.

Under RPC, programmers design distributed applications by using an interface definition language (IDL) to specify the operations that a server is to perform for clients. They then compile this definition to produce code for both client and server "stub programs". Upon execution, the client program calls the client stub on the local machine. This stub packages the arguments, transmits the data to the server, and waits for the server's reply. On the server side, the server stub unpacks the arguments, calls the application subroutine that actually does the work, packages the results, and sends the reply to the client. The results are returned to the calling program in the same way as the results of local procedure calls.

By this means, the programmer is spared concern about networking details or the architecture of remote machines. Security concerns are also addressed: RPC supports secure communication between client and server (that is, between local and remote systems).

The RPC run-time libraries will work with either the X/Open Transport Interface (XTI) or a socket interface to any of several transport protocols: TCP, UDP, DECnet, and Domain. The Network Data Representation (NDR), allowing a choice of representations, is used to encode data, and there are no limits upon the number, type, or size of parameters in remote procedure calls. RPC supports data types from multi-byte character sets, such as those used by Japanese, Arabic, and Chinese languages, in a manner consistent with ISO standards.

A note on the term "RPC". Actually, the acronym has three distinct references in this book. In the first place, there are RPCs associated with the NFS operating system (§6.9). OSF/1 supports these "NFS RPCs" so far as is necessary to implement NFS, but not for general use by the programmer. Secondly, there are RPCs provided by the Mach message facilities of OSF/1. In particular, the **msg_rpc** system call (§3.2) is a means for remote procedure execution. Thirdly, the RPCs discussed in this section are a part of DCE, and are distinct in implementation from the other two varieties.

For a more detailed discussion of DCE remote procedure calls, see the OSF white paper reprinted in Appendix A.

13.8

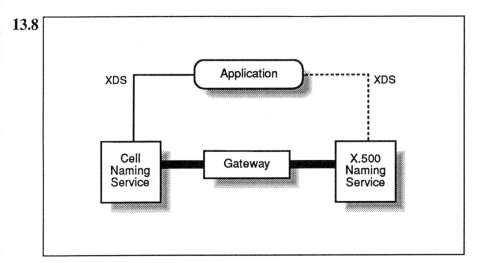

Naming service

The naming, or directory, service maps user-understandable names to internal representations stored in a distributed database. The objects named include such things as countries, organizations, persons, groups, organizational roles, computers, printers, files, processes, and application services together with their interfaces. The clients of the naming service range from other DCE services to applications such as print spoolers and mailers.

The naming service allows you to identify an object regardless of that object's location on the network or the path required to reach it. Further, by means of replication—maintaining copies of the database on multiple servers—naming information is kept available despite partial failure of the network. And because names you look up are "cached" on your machine for use in later lookup, much of the need for network traffic is eliminated.

For performance reasons, updates to the name database are not automatically posted to every replica and cache; this updating occurs only at intervals selected by the administrator.

Gateways and X.500. Every cell (§13.4) has its own naming service. In addition, DCE supports the X.500 directory protocols, making an X.500 name server directly accessible to programs. As a result, the application program uses a common interface to access either cell or remote names. This interface, developed by X/Open and called X/Open Directory Service (XDS), is modeled on—but not restricted to—X.500 directory services. To clients of the X.500 server, names managed by the cell naming service are viewed as a "directory management domain".

The DCE naming service includes clients, servers, management tools, replication daemons, and programming interfaces based on XDS. In addition, it provides a cell/world gateway, and a gateway to the Internet Domain Name Service.

For a more detailed discussion of the name service, see the OSF white paper reprinted in Appendix B.

13.9

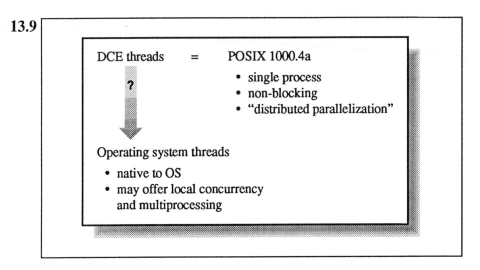

Threads in a distributed computing environment

Parallelism does not necessarily imply multiple processors in a single computer. If a program is executing in a distributed computing environment, it can achieve parallelism by simultaneously exploiting multiple computing resources across a network. The DCE threads service allows a single program to execute concurrently on more than one machine. For example, while one program thread carries out a remote procedure call, another might handle user input.

The efficiency gain in such an approach is not negated when the program is invoked on a uniprocessor machine. It will happen that the threads execute one at a time—alternately—on this machine, but as soon as one of the threads takes advantage of resources elsewhere on the network, true concurrency results. And even without going out over the network, threads on a uniprocessor system offer many of the advantages of multiple processes; for example, if one thread blocks, say, on an I/O request, a second thread can continue executing.

Such techniques, useful in client applications, are especially important in servers, which typically must handle requests from several clients at the same time.

It is important to note, however, that threads in this sense are not the same as threads native to an operating system—such as the Mach threads discussed earlier in this book (§2.1). Rather, the DCE threads service provides a higher-level mechanism that may or may not be "mapped" to the native threads (if they exist) of a particular operating system. This mapping occurs via small wrapper routines that translate DCE's POSIX 1003.4a-compliant thread semantics to the operating system's built-in thread semantics. An application using DCE threads need not know whether it is running on a machine with native threads, or whether it is running on a machine with more than one processor.

DCE threads—when they are not mapped to native operating system threads—run as co-routines in a single process executing in user address space. The package provides synchronization primitives, a variety of scheduling policies, and thread preemption and cancelation facilities.

13.10

> **Security**
> - Kerberos authentication
> - Access control lists
> - User registry
> - Secure messages via RPC

Security services

Security issues are accentuated in a distributed computing environment. Whereas, in a single, time-sharing computer, the operating system verifies the identity of users and services, and keeps a record of permissions, who is to assess the validity of a claim on resources coming from a remote system? The requirements here are several:

Authentication. Identify users and services; block forgeries.

Authorization. Grant appropriate access rights and other privileges. For example, a file server must be able to determine whether a user is authorized to read a given file.

Message integrity and privacy. Avoid forgeries; guarantee the privacy of messages upon request.

The need for authentication is met by the already widely distributed Kerberos software from MIT's Project Athena, which has been integrated into the broader DCE security package.

Authorization is based on POSIX-conforming access control lists, combining seven different access rights that can be assigned on both an individual and group basis. In addition, a "user registry" ensures the use of unique user names and passwords across the distributed network, checks the accuracy and consistency of this information, and provides security for updates and changes. It maintains a single, logical database of user account information, including user and group naming information, login account information, and general system properties and policies.

Message integrity is guaranteed by facilities (integrated with RPC) for detecting when a message has been altered or corrupted. Encryption yields privacy.

Such distributed security mechanisms can be used in combination with any security features found in the underlying operating system. But there is no system of ratings such as B1 or C2, since distributed system security is currently outside the scope of guidelines such as the *U.S. Department of Defense Trusted Computer System Evaluation* (the "orange book").

Security exacts performance penalties. Therefore application programmers and administrators are given the ability to choose different levels of security. A privilege server allows the addition or removal of specific privileges under controlled conditions.

For a more detailed discussion of security services, see the OSF white paper reprinted in Appendix C.

13.11

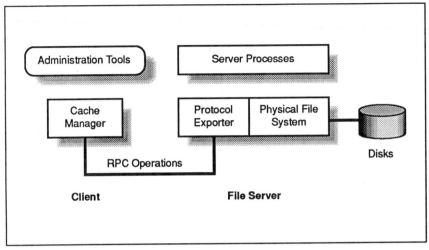

Distributed file system

A distributed files system extends the idea of a file system—once restricted to an individual computer—to embrace files on several, or perhaps thousands, of computers. The distinction between local and remote files tends to disappear.

The de facto standard for distributed file systems has been NFS, or Network File System, from Sun Microsystems. NFS is supported by OSF/1. However, believing NFS to be possessed of certain weaknesses, OSF selected the Andrew File System (AFS) from Transarc for use in DCE. The developers at OSF point at the following strengths in AFS:

- It incorporates a more complete implementation of the file access and sharing semantics specified in the POSIX 1003.1a standard, Portable Operating System Interface.

- Users can specify files with the same pathname from anywhere in a network, with no distinction between local and remote files.

- The complexity of the distributed file system is hidden from system managers. For each cell (§13.4), only one administrator is needed for management, monitoring, and maintenance. Online file backup tools are provided.

- Access control mechanisms protect the objects (files and directories) by enforcing uniformity inside a cell. Appropriate security mechanisms for connections to other cells are also provided.

- All accessible data resources are maximally available. Access to files and directories inside a cell is not interrupted by single server failures. Replicated units ("filesets") of file systems are available on a read-only basis.

- The file server can respond to a large number of concurrent requests with adequate performance. Sections of files can be cached on client machines.

- The file server is designed to work in a wide area network.

The distributed file system supports diskless workstations by using the cache manager on client systems. The operation of this diskless virtual memory model is distinct from the virtual memory implementation on the underlying operating system—although vendors supplying DCE may choose to take advantage of the native virtual memory.

In addition to the POSIX 1003.1a standard, the distributed file system:

- provides discretionary access control in conformance with POSIX 1003.6 Security Interface (using access control lists)

- complies with the Internet BOOTP (bootstrap) and TFTP (trivial file transfer) protocols for booting diskless workstations

- allows NFS and (PC)NFS clients to interact with the file system, by means of the AFS and NFS protocol exporter (see figure)

Finally, the physical file system, designed to support file servers, is based on logical partitions (filesets) that can be configured independently of the underlying physical partitions. These filesets are the entities affected by administrative functions such as replication, reconfiguration (moving subtrees, or directory hierarchies), and backup. The physical file system is log-based, which offers advantages for restart and recovery after a crash.

For a more detailed discussion of the distributed file system, see the OSF white paper reprinted in Appendix D.

13.12

> PCs (MS-DOS, OS/2) can have
>
> - network file access
> - network printer access
>
> PC client software is not supplied by OSF, but is being developed by independent vendors

Personal computer integration

Personal computer integration gives minicomputer, mainframe, and PC users the ability to share files, peripherals, and applications. However, DCE supplies the required server functions on the non-PC systems only. The necessary client software to complete the integration depends on the PC vendors.

Given the necessary PC-side clients, personal computer integration supports these functions:

File support. Users of PCs (MS-DOS and OS/2-based personal computers) can view, copy, and move files to and from the distributed file system.

Remote printing support. PCs can share the server's printers so as to print files stored locally or on the server. Users can control the routing carried out by print spooling and print queue management services.

Miscellaneous capabilities. PC integration *may* include application program interfaces (APIs) between MS_DOS and UNIX systems, electronic mail, remote execution on UNIX systems, and terminal emulation.

The PC integration services incorporate elements from two different products. On the one hand, they include the Sun Microsystems (PC)NFS interface and protocol, endorsed by the *X/Open Portability Guide* (XPG4). On the other hand, they support the Server Message Block file and print service protocol that is part of the LAN Manager/X product from Hewlett-Packard and Microsoft.

A

REMOTE PROCEDURE CALL

in a Distributed Computing Environment

An OSF White Paper

IN THIS CHAPTER

Developments in computer hardware have steadily increased the share of computing resources available to an individual user. When commercial computing was prevalent, in the 1950s and 1960s, computers were single-user resources. *Batch* systems then were developed to take better advantage of the central processing unit. Next came *timesharing* systems, which allowed a large number of users to interact with a single CPU. *Workstation* networks evolved from timesharing systems, letting users carry out applications without sharing a CPU—thus gaining the performance that technical applications require. In the mid-1980s, system vendors introduced *network file systems,* which made it easy for people to share information, allowing workstations to export their file systems through the network.

Distributed computing is the next evolutionary step beyond file sharing. A *distributed computing environment* makes a collection of loosely connected systems appear to be a single entity. Distributed computing makes it easy to develop and run applications that use computing resources throughout a network. Individual programs within an application can be distributed to computers best suited for the task. Tasks that can run in parallel are easily distributed to multiple computers at once, providing higher performance for users and better utilization of computing resources throughout the network.

From an applications point of view, a single computer that could handle all the needs of the user would be ideal, but the trend in hardware evolution is to provide many specialized computers instead of a single general-purpose system. A distributed computing environment, on the other hand, can function as a single large computer. Typically, a distributed computing environment functions in a heterogeneous environment, one that contains different types of computer systems.

The OSF Distributed Computing Environment (DCE) allows applications—file systems, backup servers, database applications, and a countless variety of user-defined applications—to run over a heterogeneous network. The basic technology that enables such operation is the *remote procedure call,* or RPC.

The Remote Procedure Call Model

The RPC model is based on a simple proposition: make individual procedures in an application run on a computer elsewhere on the network. The RPC presents to the application developer a familiar programming construct, the procedure call, and generalizes this capability from a single system to a network of systems. RPCs are highly suitable for networks in which clients—users or applications—request services from network servers, that is, computers that supply requested services. For example, a long-running numerical application that contains a computationally complex procedure can take advantage of RPCs. Its total time-to-solution could be reduced by running the time-consuming procedure on a high-speed compute server.

Another class of applications that can benefit from client/server RPCs are database applications. For example, a company may have an online corporate database consisting of its employees' names, telephone extensions, and department numbers. This database could be copied to each user's system. Alternatively, by having only one copy of a database on the network that can be accessed by remote procedure calls, valuable disk space on client systems can be freed for other purposes. Furthermore, this approach prevents the horrendous problem of periodically updating multiple database copies to make them consistent.

RPCs provide programmers with a number of powerful tools necessary to build client/server applications. They include two major components:

- A language and a compiler that simplify the development of distributed applications by producing portable source code that allows remote procedure calls to behave as local procedure calls.

- A run-time facility that allows distributed applications to run over multiple, heterogeneous systems, thus making the systems architectures, and the underlying *network transport protocols* connecting the systems, transparent to the application procedures.

IDL Compiler

In the early days of computer programming, applications were written without regard to an internal structure, thus making application code hard to follow and maintain. Subsequently, structured programming techniques organized applications into procedures that performed specialized tasks (for example, accessing a record from a database; multiplying two matrices and putting the results in a third matrix) with well defined interfaces. Much like a matching electrical outlet and plug, the interfaces specify the data and parameters to be passed between procedures (for instance, input "a" and "b" and return the results into "c").

In distributed applications development, the programmer creates an *interface definition* in an interface definition language (IDL). The DCE IDL syntax is similar to ANSI C, a language familiar to most programmers, and therefore is easy to use even by novice distributed application developers. The DCE IDL has additional language constructs appropriate for a network environment. For example, the *autobind* attribute specifies the remote procedure to identify, locate, and bind to an alternate server should the server on which it is running fail.

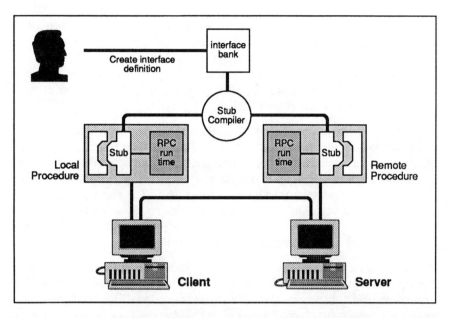

Figure A-1. The application developer creates an interface definition for a distributed application. The IDL compiler translates the interface definition code into stubs that are bound with the local and remote procedures on the client and server side, respectively. The stubs work with the RPC run-time facility, which provides system-level support for RPC operations.

The DCE IDL *compiler* translates the IDL interface definition into stubs that are bound with the client and server (see Figure 1). The stub on the client side *stands in* for the server procedure. Similarly, the stub on the server side *stands in* for the client procedure. These stubs facilitate remote procedure calls by doing what a programmer would otherwise write by hand: copying arguments to and from RPC packets, converting data representations (as necessary), and calling the RPC run time.

In a heterogeneous environment, different machines may represent data differently. Making a remote procedure call introduces a new complexity: translating a procedure's data from one machine format to another. For example, the order of bytes within an integer on an IBM system is different from the order on a Motorola 680x0 system. Rather than requiring the application developer to perform the translation, the DCE IDL compiler carries out this function.

Many RPC systems use a *canonical* form, or a defined format, for data representation; this means of communication is comparable to a German and a French person conversing in English. Unless the client's native data representation is the same as the canonical form, it must convert data to the canonical format. The same holds true for the server. The drawback to this scheme occurs when the client and server share the same native representation that is not the same as the canonical format. This requires two unnecessary data conversions for every variable passed in every call (with two more conversions for every variable returned to the caller). This redundancy is similar to requiring two persons whose native language is French to converse in English.

To overcome this shortcoming, the DCE RPC uses an innovative approach to data representation. In this scheme, all calls are tagged by the RPC mechanism with a description of the calling machine's basic data representations (for example, how integers, characters, and floating-point data are represented; this information can be captured in fewer than four bytes). When the call is received, the receiver converts the data from the sender's representation to the receiver's representation. The conversion occurs only when the descriptor tags denote that the sending and receiving machines represent data differently.

The DCE approach to data conversion is generally the preferable choice. Because work groups or departments typically have the same type of computing equipment, RPCs between systems with the same data representation can be expected to represent a large fraction of the calls made, even in a heterogeneous network. These calls should not be burdened with an unnecessary performance penalty.

Some experts argue that the direct data conversion approach bogs down in heterogeneous networks with many different data representations. However, the actual number of different data representations that a server must handle in a distributed computing environment is fairly small; the computer industry is clearly converging on a few standard options. In representing string data, for example, most computers use either ASCII or EBCDIC format.

Still, in some cases the canonical approach may be superior. The DCE RPC supports the negotiation of data representation schemes so that additional ones such as the ISO/Abstract Syntax Notation Basic Encoding Rules (ASN.1 BER) can be incorporated and used by developers.

RPC Run Time

Once a distributed application has been developed, and the client and server stubs are compiled and linked, it still must run over the network. The RPC run-time facility provides the mechanisms for transferring requests from the clients to the servers and transmitting and receiving responses over the network. The DCE RPC run time also interacts with other DCE services on the network, such as naming, security, and time services.

For the run-time facility to be practical in the commercial world, it must have the following features and characteristics.

- It should be *transparent* and *independent* of any network on which it runs. This means that the run-time facility can be ported to run over any network without affecting the behavior of applications. Developers need not rewrite applications for different networks.

- The run-time facility also must allow the distributed application to run reliably over the network. It must recover cleanly from failures on the client or server side, and in the network between the systems.

- The run-time facility must support file systems, databases, and other services and applications that send and receive variable-length data.

- It must provide a common method for network *naming* or *directory* services, which should allow access to services over the network by a name easily used by humans, rather than by an obscure network address. The RPC facility must be independent of any one directory service.

- The run-time facility must interact with a *secure* facility that protects communications from tampering. A security service must ensure the *privacy* of confidential information and protect the *integrity* of communications. The RPC facility must be independent of any one security service.

- The run-time facility also must support *multithreading* for *concurrent* or parallel processing on the network, allowing an application to perform many actions simultaneously. Multithreading allows a server to handle multiple requests efficiently and simultaneously, thus reducing the time required to complete an application. Multithreading also should allow cancelation of operations in progress without terminating the entire service.

- The run-time facility must be designed for portability to and interoperability with system environments from multiple vendors.

- The run-time facility must track RPC standards as they emerge. Doing so ensures interoperability on a wide variety of vendor platforms. The run-time facility should be designed to allow introduction of new protocols without requiring changes to existing applications.

Network Independence and Transparency

The DCE RPC provides both transport independence *and* transparency. Transport independence refers to the RPC's ability to run over any wide or local area network. Mere network independence, however, is insufficient to ensure that applications run consistently over any transport. An RPC also must provide network transparency for its features to work over all transports, and for the distributed application code to act identically, regardless of the network on which the application runs. By eliminating the need to change application code for each given underlying network, the DCE RPC significantly reduces the time required for application development.

An issue related to network transparency is *at-most-once semantics.* Some remote procedures may have no "side effects" on a database or on the state of the data used by the application procedure, regardless of whether the procedure is executed once, or many times. These are known as *idempotent* procedures. For example, a remote procedure that writes a person's new address into a file may be executed once or may be inadvertently written many times and not corrupt the file. On the other hand, a procedure to subtract $100 from an individual's bank account changes the state of the data each time it is executed. It is necessary to ensure that, should the network connection fail and later restart during the remote call, the latter class of procedures execute no more than once. The DCE RPC ensures correct operation through at-most-once semantics and high performance through idempotent semantics.

Some RPCs depend on reliable transports to ensure that remote procedures are executed at most once. However, because the RPC must be independent of the underlying transport, it cannot rely on such services being available. An RPC that places responsibility on the application developer to be aware of the limitations of the underlying transport, and develop distributed applications accordingly, is insufficient. For that reason the DCE RPC is independent of the underlying transport, freeing the application developer to concentrate on the application.

One aspect of the application in which the developer must concentrate is its semantics, i.e., how the application behaves. The RPC run-time facility cannot make assumptions about the applications, e.g., it cannot assume that a procedure can execute more than once without harmful side effects (such as the debit-bank-account procedure). Only the application writer is in a position to know the semantics of a given operation. The DCE allows the developer to specify the semantics, and the RPC guarantees that they will work correctly on any transport.

Reliability

In traditional, single systems, applications may be designed to recover cleanly from system failures. Graceful recovery is also desirable in distributed applications. In a network environment, unfortunately, more things can go wrong: for example, the client and/or server could fail. The network between the systems also could fail.

The DCE RPC is designed to run reliably in the face of lost messages, duplicated messages, long-delayed messages, messages arriving out of order, server crashes, and other problems to which networks are prone. Some networks may implement these reliability features. However, as discussed in the previous section on network independence and transparency, the DCE RPC is independent of the underlying transport. Hence, it does not depend on such reliability services being available.

Pipe Mechanism

Due to client or server resource limitations, such as inadequate main memory, an application may better handle large amounts of typed data in smaller chunks while maintaining the structure of the data. The DCE RPC includes a pipe facility that efficiently sends and receives indeterminate-length streams, or chunks, of typed bulk data. Pipes are useful for a diverse range of applications, such as database services and file systems, which require efficient handling of bulk data. The DCE file system, for example, uses the RPC pipe facility to efficiently move large, variable-sized chunks of data to and from remote files.

Directory Services

A *directory* service allows users to identify network resources such as servers, files, disks, or print queues, and allows RPCs to access them by name, without needing to know their location in a network. Integrating the RPC with a highly available directory service is a fundamental characteristic of a distributed system architecture. In a dynamically changing distributed computing environment, a directory service tracks the location of a service that may change from time to time. Consumers of these services cannot rely on presumptions about their existence or location, but must consult a dynamic registry. When users rely solely on a directory service for accessing objects, the directory server must remain available in the face of partial network failures. The DCE Directory Service seam-

lessly integrates the RPC with an X.500 global directory system and a fast, replicated local directory system.

For high availability, users also may replicate the remote procedure onto many
servers on the network. Hence, a procedure might talk to a different server each
time it is invoked. Hard coding or "wiring" the location of the remote service
into the calling procedure clearly would be cumbersome in such an environment
because it requires the encoding of a new location every time a new instance of
the procedure is added to or deleted from the network, or modified in any way.
With the DCE Directory Service, each time a procedure is invoked, it can make a
directory server call to find the address of the object's server and the communications protocol required to access the server. The procedure thus can obtain all the
information it needs to issue an RPC call to bind to the remote object.

In many instances, finding an object using attributes rather than a text name
proves more convenient. The DCE Directory Service provides this ability. Thus,
a client can query the directory service for a list of "6 page/sec laser printers"
rather than requiring the application developer to manage the mapping between
machine names and attributes.

For a more detailed discussion of directory services, please see the OSF white
paper *Directory Services for a Distributed Computing Environment*.

Security

In most conventional timesharing systems, the operating system *authenticates* the
identity of users and controls access to resources. In a distributed computing
environment, however, this task falls to independent security services. In a small,
closed distributed environment, a procedure running on one machine can assume
that the messages it receives over the network come from a known, *trusted*
source.

This may not be a safe assumption in a large, multi-location, open distributed
computing environment that may be open to eavesdropping or vulnerable to network "viruses." In such an environment, it may be necessary for the client to
authenticate its identity to the server, and demonstrate that it is *authorized,* or has
permission, to use the requested service. One solution to this problem involves
the sharing of a mutual secret between *principals,* (clients and servers)—a private key that cannot be known by other principals.

In the OSF DCE, a security service makes an RPC request to the security server
(the trusted source) to create a *ticket* for use between principals. The ticket contains encrypted authentication information that the two principals exchange. By
doing so, they demonstrate to one another that each has proven its identity to the

trusted service. The trusted service then grants a common unique key used to encrypt all communications between the principals to ensure data privacy and integrity. Once the principals are authenticated, an authorization mechanism can be used to control access to resources.

For a more detailed discussion of security, please see the OSF white paper *Security in a Distributed Computing Environment.*

Concurrent Processing

Humans are very good at performing multiple operations simultaneously, talking on the telephone while reading the newspaper, for example. *Concurrent processing* is a way of allowing PCs, workstations, and desktop computers to do the same. For instance, it permits a computer to print one file while editing another.

Concurrent processing uses a collection of lightweight *tasks* within a *process*, or single address space. Lightweight tasks are more efficient than processes because they take up less overhead. A task, such as printing or editing, is a *thread* of execution—a single flow of control. In a synchronous thread of execution, a calling procedure waits for the receiving procedure to return the requested results.

Having multiple threads in a program means that at any one instant the program has multiple points of execution, one in each of its threads. The execution of each thread is *asynchronous;* that is, one thread need not wait for another to complete its execution. In a distributed computing environment, shared network servers, such as a print server, can service requests from multiple clients. Use of multiple threads allows the server to handle clients' requests in parallel, instead of serializing them (or creating one server process per client, an expensive proposition). With threads, a server may handle one client while another is blocked.

Threads with RPCs make a potentially powerful combination. A client can issue multiple RPC calls to search multiple remote distributed databases concurrently. Network backup-and-restore servers can handle multiple clients in parallel, provided there is an effective mechanism for multiplexing data to and from the multiple sources. Distributed expert systems can use many RPCs to span decision trees in parallel to arrive at a conclusion quickly. Matrix reduction and other computational tasks can be distributed to multiple machines at once, in effect turning the network into a large, parallel multiprocessing supercomputer.

Along with concurrency comes responsibility to ensure that the operations of tasks do not interfere with each other. For example, applications that access shared data must be very careful to avoid errors arising when two threads attempt to change the same data in a file simultaneously, or in the wrong order. Mutex (mutual exclusion) locks and other tools solve this problem.

The OSF DCE offers a powerful, highly portable threads package integrated with the DCE RPC. The threads service is based on the POSIX draft specification 1003.4a, expected to be final in 1991.

Openness and Portability

The DCE RPC is based on an openly specified architecture that provides a common base for the independent development of distributed computing products, applications, and services. Unlike RPC implementations that allow for "customization code," the DCE RPC specification definitively describes the RPC protocol. As a result, DCE RPC works consistently from one vendor's implementation to another, thus ensuring interoperability between those systems.

Standards

In addition to openness and portability, adherence to standards facilitates interoperability in heterogeneous networks. The DCE is well positioned to respond to developments in international standards. Although no ISO RPC standard exists, the latest drafts of an ECMA (European Computer Manufacturers Association) RPC standard and ANSI (American National Standards Institute) RPC requirements indicate that the DCE IDL is well positioned and consistent with the future ISO interface definition language. In addition, the modular design of the DCE RPC stub/run-time interface permits introduction of a new RPC protocol based on ISO services (such as ROSE, or Remote Operations Service Elements) with no changes to existing applications.

An RPC Case Study: The Putnam Companies

The Putnam Companies is an investment management firm in Boston, Massachusetts. Its use of an RPC facility illustrates the benefits of distributed computing environments. Until recently, fund managers had no automated means of obtaining information and collecting it in one computer. The most up-to-date information they could obtain was day-old hardcopy.

To resolve this problem, Putnam undertook a software project to create the Financial Workbench. The Financial Workbench is a set of tools that support the rapid development of financial applications software by providing programmers with a set of object definitions for financial objects, and network transparent access to many data sources and services through the use of Network Computing System (NCS) RPC facility, on which OSF's DCE RPC is based.

The Financial Workbench defines various objects and associated operations performed on those objects. Figure 2 shows a simple example of how the Financial Workbench can be used to obtain the current price of IBM stock (i.e., the market quotation operation on the IBM stock object). The current market quotation is one of several possible operations that may be applied to the IBM stock object. For example, to plot the trend of IBM stock over time, historical prices on IBM stock may be accessed by time series operations provided by an historical time series server.

Putnam has implemented the Financial Workbench on Apollo and Sun workstations, DECstation systems, VAX systems and PC compatibles. Although not currently part of the Financial Workbench, a threads package could be incorporated to allow for multiple concurrent inquiries for whole portfolios of securities. The Financial Workbench allows new applications to build quickly to meet the ever-changing information requirements of funds managers. Before the existence of the Financial Workbench, Putnam's portfolio managers had no financial applications. With the Financial Workbench, they have access to integrated tools. Now they can more easily tap into their network to gain access to data to make more timely buy/sell decisions, thus improving the financial performance of the securities portfolios they manage.

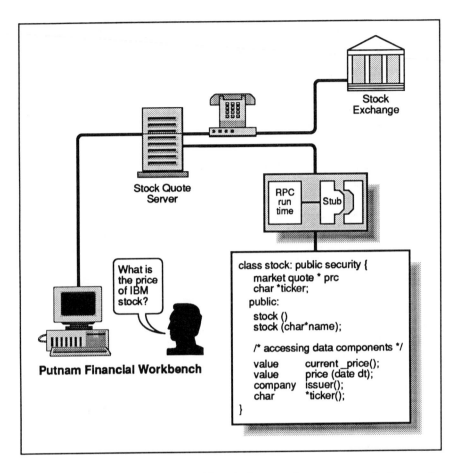

Figure A-2. Putnam Financial Workbench shows an investment analyst accessing the IBM stock price. The application makes a remote procedure call to the stock-quote server to determine the current market value of the stock.

Summary

The DCE RPC provides a combination of capabilities and features not available from other RPCs today. They include:

- A compiler that simplifies the development of distributed applications.

- A run-time facility that provides network independence and transparency, allowing a distributed application to run over any network, and eliminating the need to rewrite the application for different network transport services.

- Efficient handling of bulk data, enabling a diverse range of applications to use RPC functions.

- Efficient data presentation services, eliminating unnecessary data translation between like machines.

- Integration with directory services, allowing easy and highly available access to distributed services throughout the network.

- Integration with security, protecting the privacy and integrity of data sent to, or received from, remote procedures.

- Integration with threads, allowing remote procedures to run in parallel over the network, reducing the time to complete the application.

- Modular architecture, allowing integration with alternative directory (or naming), security, threads, and other services that may be added in the future.

- Portable code, which promotes widespread commercial availability of distributed applications.

The computer industry stands at the threshold of an exciting new era—the era of distributed computing. This technology unites a network of diverse computers into a single entity at the command of the user. As a result, users can take advantage of new technology while protecting investments in current equipment and skills. RPC technology greatly simplifies the distribution of applications, thus more effectively harnessing the diverse computational horsepower inherent in networks.

B

DIRECTORY SERVICES

for a Distributed Computing Environment

An OSF White Paper

IN THIS CHAPTER

- Clients and Servers

- The Need for Naming In a Distributed Environment

- OSF DCE Directory Service

- Availability

- Security

- Manageability

- Performance and Extensibility

- Integration with Specialized Directory Services

- X.500 Global Directory Service

- XDS Application Programming Interface

- Conclusion

Computer networking is undergoing tremendous change. Personal computers and workstations are connected directly to local area networks, which, in turn, are interconnected via high-speed global networks. The potential now exists for any computer to communicate with millions of others—anywhere in the world.

With these advanced communications capabilities come complications—for the end user, system administrator, and application developer. They require a computing environment that will allow them to fully exploit the rich potential of the network without having to contend with its underlying complexity. What is needed is a means of masking the intricacies of the network while providing optimal communications capability.

In 1990, the Open Software Foundation announced its selection of technologies for an environment that would meet those needs: the OSF Distributed Computing Environment (DCE). This offering is a set of integrated technologies that together provide a powerful and easy-to-use means of constructing distributed network applications and services that meet the needs of today's computing environments. The DCE includes communication, distributed file service, identification and location, time service, and network security technologies.

At the heart of OSF's DCE is the directory (or name) service, the component that allows users and programs to locate and describe people, places, applications, and services that participate in the distributed computing environment. Naming is a key ingredient in distributed computing because it helps people manage the information that is available through the network.

This paper describes the OSF DCE directory service. The beginning describes what names are, how the OSF DCE makes use of names, and the motivation for developing a distributed directory service. The remainder of the paper discusses how the DCE directory service meets those needs, describing its operation and key benefits.

Clients and Servers

Distributed services operate by allowing a user on a computer connected to a network to access information on another computer. The computer on which the user is working is called the *client*. The computer on which the information is stored is called the *server*. This model of distributed computing is appropriately called the *client/server model*.

The Need for Naming In a Distributed Environment

People depend on names to identify and describe things. Names convey a great deal of information, such as physical attributes. The name house, for instance, connotes a structure that may have four walls, a roof, a door, and a window.

Names and information about the things they describe can be collected into lists and made publicly available so that people can reference this information. For example, the names of people and organizations are compiled in telephone directories that provide such information as telephone numbers and street addresses. In a geographically dispersed society, telephone directories provide an efficient, easy-to-use method of locating people. Telephone directories also allow people to be found after they move. When people move within a city, their new address and telephone number are listed with their name in an updated edition of the telephone directory.

Computer networks likewise require names and directories to describe and record the characteristics of the diverse services and information they provide. For example, an electronic mail system must be able to locate a user's mailbox in order to deliver his mail. The mail delivery application contacts another application, called a *directory* or *name service,* to look up the user's name and indicate the location of his mail box.

In a distributed computing environment, anything that can be accessed individually and given a name is called an *object.* Examples of objects are network services, electronic mailboxes, and computers. Each object has a corresponding listing in the directory service called an *entry,* which contains information, or *attributes,* that describe the objects. Name entries can be collected into lists of entries called *directories.* For example, in a telephone directory, the listings are the entries, and the location information, such as the telephone number or street address, represents attributes of these entries.

Attributes can be any type of information that describes an object, such as location, color, or size. For instance, regular telephone directories contain only location-specific attributes, such as a street address. Business telephone directories include additional attributes such as the hours of operation and types of credit cards accepted.

The name service allows directories to be organized into hierarchies in which a directory can contain other directories. For instance, an international telephone directory contains country telephone directories. The country directories, in turn, contain provincial directories, which contain city directories. The city directories contain actual name listings.

The name service is central to the distributed computing environment because objects are defined by their names. Applications and services gain access to an object first by accessing its name entry and retrieving its attributes. Decoupling the location or access characteristics of an object from the object itself is called *location independence.* It allows the applications and services to access an object even when the object moves or changes other vital characteristics such as language. For instance, the business telephone directory can tell us where a business has moved. It can also tell us that the business has changed its hours of operation.

OSF DCE Directory Service

The directory service used by the OSF Distributed Computing Environment is integrated with the other DCE components. For example, the directory service meets the performance and scaling needs of the distributed file system and is accessible by applications based on the remote procedure call component. In addition, it provides security, high availability, and compatibility with recognized naming standards.

The DCE directory service was designed to meet the needs of an integrated distributed computing environment. It is based on Digital Equipment Corporation's DECdns and Siemen's DIR-X, which had many of the same design requirements as the OSF DCE. In particular the service was designed to support networks with 100,000 to 1,000,000 computers, and to be highly available, self-configuring, fast, easy to manage, and secure. The DCE directory service meets these requirements by making use of state-of-the-art technology such as *partitioning, caching, replication, authentication* and *authorization,* and by complying with accepted naming standards, such as the X.500 worldwide directory service and the X/Open directory service programming interface.

Availability

One of the greatest advantages of a distributed computing environment is the elimination of the single point of failure that has plagued timesharing systems. The overall environment is resistant to a temporary failure of any one resource. However, failure of a resource central to all other services could affect the entire computing environment.

The directory system is central to all other applications and services in the distributed computing environment. It provides the means for all applications and services to locate and share information about objects. Therefore, it must be available at all times. The directory system must be resistant to random software and hardware failures and must be available during administrative activities. For instance, modifying entries or running backups on a database must not interfere with its normal operation.

The DCE directory service ensures high availability by distributing multiple copies of directories on many computers. This mechanism, called *replication,* allows the name service to be available if one of the server computers fails. Many of the other DCE components support replication, thus making the entire environment extremely reliable and highly available.

Replication creates an issue that must be addressed in the design of a highly available distributed directory service. The DCE directory service allows multiple copies of directories to reside on multiple computers. This can lead to inconsistency when one copy is modified and others are unchanged. The DCE directory service solves this problem by providing a sophisticated update mechanism.

Security

Distributed services require access to sensitive information about individuals. For instance, a company-wide payroll system might need such information as employees' salaries. Employees, however, typically prefer that this information is not publicly accessible. For such cases, the name service must provide a security mechanism that protects the information.

In order to protect sensitive information, a security system must solve two problems. It must prove that users and services are who they claim to be, through *authentication.* In addition, the directory service must provide a mechanism that grants access only to authorized individuals as well as distinguish between individuals who may read a name and those who also may modify it. This mechanism is called *authorization.*

The DCE directory service uses Kerberos authentication, developed by the Massachusetts Institute of Technology's Project Athena, to prove that users and services are who they claim to be. Kerberos uses a sophisticated three-party mechanism that allows authentication to be controlled from a single location. This technique is called *symmetric private key encryption.* Through the authorization feature of the directory service, an employee might be allowed to look up his current salary but be restricted from modifying it.

The DCE directory service uses access control lists to identify which individuals or groups of individuals are permitted to access a directory of names and which operations they can perform on the names. The DCE directory service affords several types of protection, thus limiting permission to create, delete, read, or modify names.

The combination of access control lists and Kerberos authentication provides a new level of security for distributed computing.

Manageability

As computer networks grow larger, maintaining an entire name service on a single computer becomes difficult. First, a single computer cannot handle the large number of naming requests likely to be made all over the world. More important, one person or authority cannot keep all the names in the world up-to-date from a single location. Consequently, many organizations find it difficult to maintain large name databases.

The US population census, for instance, is a large name database containing a list of the entire US population. Every ten years, the US census bureau surveys the population and updates this database. It takes months or years to complete this update. One way to provide frequent updates on such a database is to allow name entries to be *partitioned* onto separate but cooperating *directory servers,* which are the computers that provide name service.

Partitioning allows different directories in the name service to reside on different computers. Thus the name service can be partitioned by geographical location. For instance, the telephone directories for San Francisco can reside on servers in San Francisco, while the telephone directories for Phoenix can reside on servers in that city. This way the operation of the San Francisco directory server can be decoupled from the one in Phoenix.

Partitioning also makes the name service easier to maintain by allowing a certain measure of administrative autonomy. Because different partitions may reside on computers that are under different administrative control, they can be managed by separate authorities. A partition or collection of partitions under a single autonomous administrative authority is called an administrative *domain.* If the directory servers in San Francisco and Phoenix are part of separate administrative domains, the name entries in San Francisco can be maintained by the California Telephone Company, and the name entries in Phoenix by the Arizona Telephone Company.

Performance and Extensibility

The DCE directory service is central to the OSF distributed computing environment. For instance, the OSF DCE distributed file system uses the name service to locate files. Because of its importance to the DCE, the directory service must maintain a sufficiently high level of performance to support network services and applications.

The directory service also must scale well. It must be capable of providing excellent performance independent of the number of users or name entries. Enterprise-wide computing environments can have tens of thousands of personal computers accessing hundreds of thousands of objects. A directory system must be able to handle such a complex environment.

Many services and applications rely on the directory service for storage of all types of information. The DCE directory service improves the performance for name lookups by allowing clients to make local copies of names. This process, called *caching,* improves performance by reducing the number of times a client must go to the network for naming information. Caching works in the following way. When a client looks up a name and is returned the location of an object and its associated attributes, the name is said to be cached. The client can store this name information locally, thus obviating the need to contact the directory server on the next lookup of the same name. The cached copy of a name entry is maintained locally until an application deletes it, usually after it attempts to contact the named object and fails.

Partitioning the directory service onto separate computers and allowing directories to be replicated also improves performance and extensibility by spreading the directory service load across a number of computers and networks. For instance, if a server is overloaded because it contains a directory that is accessed by a large number of clients, replicating that directory will spread the load across other servers, thus improving the overall performance of the system.

Integration with Specialized Directory Services

The directory service must be capable of supporting the needs of specialized naming systems such as relational databases. Many of the applications and services in the distributed computing environment maintain their own name databases that contain information vital to other applications and services. Often these databases contain names and attributes of network objects that could be incorporated in the directory service.

For instance, the telephone company might have a specialized telephone directory stored in a relational database that it wishes to make publicly available. The obvious way of doing so is to create a name in the directory service for each entry in the telephone directory. This approach causes problems when the telephone directory changes and the name entries become outdated. The DCE directory service provides a mechanism that allows specialized databases to incorporate their database entries in the directory service. This mechanism, called a *junction,* allows clients to access the specialized database through the DCE directory service. Junctions consist of two pieces. The first is a communication interface that enables the specialized database to respond to clients making directory service requests. The second is a special name entry in the directory service that refers clients to the specialized database.

The communication interface that allows the specialized database to respond to directory service requests is implemented using the DCE remote procedure call (RPC) mechanism. The DCE directory service uses RPC as its standard communication interface. All clients communicate with the directory service using RPC. Because the specialized database uses this same RPC communication interface, it appears to the clients as an integral part of the directory service.

Basing the DCE directory service on DCE RPC provides a number of benefits such as portability, security, and interoperability. The entire DCE suite of services is constructed using the DCE RPC, which allows those services to be portable. Once the RPC is running on a computer platform, it is easy to compile and run the DCE directory service. The DCE RPC also provides security through its support of authenticated secure communications. In addition, if the application is using the RPC to communicate with clients, it takes up very little overhead to provide a naming junction because it uses the same shared RPC library calls the rest of the applications use.

X.500 Global Directory Service

Today's distributed environments must be capable of allowing individuals to share information, both within the organization and worldwide. Sharing information worldwide requires a global directory service that allows applications and services to locate this information.

There are two important requirements for worldwide naming. The first is providing a mechanism that is extensible and allows a standard communication medium. The second is offering an accepted, standard way of accessing the names worldwide.

Worldwide naming standards such as CCITT X.500 allow organizations to globally share names and thus share objects. X.500 is extensible and provides a standard way of accessing names. Moreover, it has been adopted as an international standard and will be used to provide worldwide directory services. The DCE directory service is compatible with X.500 directory services.

While X.500 is emerging as the standard for the global directory service, there are many reasons to choose a separate and more efficient and functional directory service for the local environment. The DCE directory service features a very sophisticated replication mechanism that provides extremely high availability. Performance in the local environment and integration with RPC clients are other important considerations. X.500 as currently specified does not address these important considerations.

The DCE directory service is designed to participate in the X.500 worldwide directory service. It provides mechanisms that tie local users into the X.500 directory service and allows users in other parts of the world to access local names through X.500. The DCE directory service provides the capabilities and mechanisms for an organization to operate a directory service administrative domain. Within that domain, the directory service administrator has control over the location of name partitions, the level of directory replication, and the level at which a user may participate in the directory service. This DCE administrative domain is connected to other administrative domains by way of the X.500 worldwide directory service through the use of naming gateways called *global directory agents* (GDAs).

When a client in one administrative domain wishes to look up a name in another, it sends a name lookup request to its local GDA. The GDA then forwards this inter-domain name request to the worldwide X.500 directory service, which looks up the name and returns an entry to the GDA. The GDA in turn passes this entry back to the client. For example, if a client in Boston wishes to find an object in Munich, it makes a request to the local DCE directory service. The directory service recognizes that this request is outside the local domain and passes it to the X.500 GDA. The GDA then communicates with the X.500 directory service in Munich and passes the results back to the original client.

The X.500 worldwide naming system can be viewed as the umbrella shown in Figure 1. The top of the umbrella is the X.500 naming system that provides the directories high up in the hierarchy, and the bottom of the umbrella represents the directories in the DCE naming system. The GDAs, in between the two naming systems, forward requests between them.

GDAs can be constructed for compatibility with any global naming scheme. GDAs already exist for X.500 and the Internet Domain Naming System, but also could be constructed for use with the Massachusetts Institute of Technology's Hesiod naming system, or for use with Sun Microsystems' NIS system.

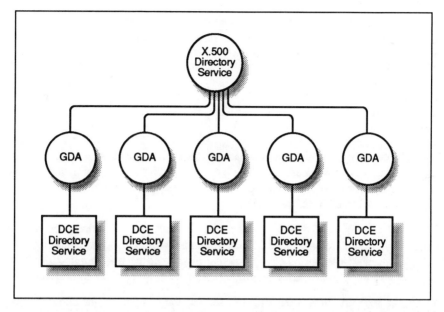

Figure B-1. X.500 provides global directory service by allowing clients in one DCE directory service administrative domain to access names in another administrative domain.

XDS Application Programming Interface

Programmers often must move applications between computing environments. In many cases, the services an application uses in one environment, such as naming services, differ from those of another environment. To limit the confusion this might present, software architects have specified service-independent *application programming interfaces* (APIs). By hiding the details of the underlying services from the applications programmer, APIs make it possible to construct applications that operate in several computing environments. In other words, as long as an application adheres to a particular API, it will operate in any environment that supports that interface.

For both the local DCE and X.500 directory services, the OSF DCE uses an API based on the X/Open Directory Service (XDS) API specification. By adhering to the XDS specification, programmers can build applications that are independent of the underlying directory service architecture. Applications that use XDS work with both the DCE and X.500 directory services without requiring changes to the software.

The DCE directory service implementation of XDS supports a rich set of functions, such as create, destroy, lookup, modify, and search. Applications that use the XDS program interface can be moved easily into the OSF DCE and operate with the DCE directory service.

Conclusion

Today's computing environment is dramatically different from the computing environment of a few years ago. The availability of personal computers, local area networks, and high-performance wide area networks has created the capability for worldwide information sharing.

The OSF Distributed Computing Environment, with its technologies for distributed file systems, remote procedure calls, and network security, provides a powerful and easy-to-use means of constructing distributed network applications and services that allow individuals and organizations to globally share information.

Central to the OSF DCE is the directory service, the component that allows applications and services to locate and refer to information in the computing environment. Its use of replication and caching provides a high level of availability, performance and scale. In addition, its use of Kerberos authentication and access control lists makes the DCE directory service secure. Moreover, the ability to partition the DCE directory service into administrative domains makes it easy to manage.

The DCE directory service supports and enhances OSF DCE by making information, available through the network, easy to find and manage.

C

SECURITY SERVICES

in a Distributed Computing Environment

An OSF White Paper

IN THIS CHAPTER

- The Need for Security in a Distributed Computing Environment
- Data Encryption Techniques
- Kerberos Authentication Using Secret Key Encryption
- Data Integrity
- Privacy of Data
- Registering Principals with DCE Registry Service
- DCE Authorization using Access Control Lists
- Conclusion

Today, users expect to reach beyond their desktops to take advantage of computing resources spread throughout their organizations. Working in distributed computing environments made up of hardware and software from different manufacturers, users are able to access data wherever it is stored on the network and bring it to the desktop — where it can be used to tackle business problems.

Distributed computing makes the most of computing resources, making them available to any user linked to those facilities by a network. With this expanded computing capability, however, come security risks. Data stored and transmitted on local and wide area networks (LANs and WANs) is vulnerable to unauthorized access, whether intentional or accidental, that could wreak havoc for businesses that rely on the integrity and confidentiality of their files. For that reason, security is a critical component in a distributed computing environment.

This paper describes the need for security in a distributed computing environment and presents a security architecture that addresses that need. In addition, it discusses an implementation of this architecture, the security component of the OSF DCE (the Distributed Computing Environment from the Open Software Foundation). DCE is the industry's only set of integrated distributed computing components for open systems.

The Need for Security in a Distributed Computing Environment

Office computers connected in networks enable people to easily and inexpensively share resources. Unfortunately, the technology that makes these networks cost-effective also makes them susceptible to eavesdropping and intrusion. Computer networks are implemented by connecting two or more computers with a common communications channel, usually a piece of wire. Because all computers in such schemes are connected to one common cable, a user of a computer connected to the network can eavesdrop easily on communications intended for another computer. Likewise, a computer can be made to "impersonate" another computer and grant a user unauthorized access to data.

The purpose of a computer security system is to allow authorized computer users to access resources in a distributed computing environment securely and confidentially. Controlling such access to information is a tricky problem. Anyone can gain access to the computer network; therefore, a method of distinguishing between computer services and users that may be trusted and those that may not is critical. For this reason both users and services must be capable of proving their identities to each other. Any entity on a computer network that is capable of proving its identity — such as a user, client, or server — is called a *unit of trust* or a *principal*.

In a distributed computing environment, security mechanisms are used to solve these problems. The security system provides *authentication systems* that allow users and resources to identify themselves so they may trust one another. It also ensures data integrity by providing mechanisms that can detect when data has been altered during transmission. An *authorization mechanism* grants authorized users access to resources and rejects requests from unauthorized users.

The OSF DCE provides an architecture that addresses the needs for a secure computing environment. The security component of DCE is integrated with the DCE remote procedure call mechanism. Together they offer application programmers and end users several levels of security including high-level data privacy, in which all network data is protected and can be viewed only by the intended recipient, as well as the option of choosing no security.

The OSF DCE security service makes use of *Kerberos authentication*, which allows principals to identify and trust one another. Kerberos uses *secret key encryption*, which allows confidential data to be sent through the network without being compromised. DCE security makes use of *cryptographic checksum* techniques that ensure data integrity by allowing corrupted data to be detected easily. In addition, DCE security provides the *DCE Registry Service*, which allows system administrators to easily manage the database of valid principals, and a distributed *access control mechanism* that allows users and administrators to control access to resources. The remainder of this paper discusses the DCE security architecture and its implementation.

Data Encryption Techniques

Network data is vulnerable to unauthorized access and tampering because it is shipped through a communications link, such as a piece of wire, or microwave transmissions. Without much difficulty, someone could tap into the communications link and monitor information being transmitted. One way to protect network data is to scramble it in a way that can be reversed only by those parties intended to receive it.

The scrambling technique used in secure communication is called *encryption*. A message is encrypted, or encoded, in a way that can be reversed only with the appropriate password, or *secret key*. Developed during the early days of the Roman Empire, encryption techniques make use of complicated mathematics. In the secret decoder rings offered by advertisers in early radio programs, for example, a number was substituted for each letter in the alphabet. The set of numbers needed to decode a message made up the key. The operation of substituting the numbers for the letters is the *encryption algorithm*. Consequently, computer encryption can be described as a mathematical method of locking information in an impenetrable box that can be opened only with the correct mathematical key.

Secret decoder rings used simple encryption techniques. In comparison, today's encryption algorithms are very sophisticated and cannot be decoded without a secret key.

Kerberos Authentication Using Secret Key Encryption

The OSF DCE makes use of the Kerberos authentication service from the Massachusetts Institute of Technology's Project Athena. Kerberos uses a sophisticated authentication mechanism that meets the requirements of open computer networks.

Kerberos requires principals to exchange secret messages that prove their identities to each other. A scenario from the world of international espionage, in which one secret agent must pass microfilm containing top-secret information to another agent, demonstrates how this authentication scheme works.

The two agents meet on a dark corner in Gorky Park. Before carrying out their mission, however, they must ascertain each other's identity. Unlike ordinary citizens, the agents do not depend on written credentials such as passports, which can be forged or stolen. Such documents have no credence in the spy world. For that reason, the spies exchange secret messages.

"The moon is in the fourth quarter," says one agent. The other responds, "Yes, it's a beautiful night for a dance." Through that exchange, the spies verify each other's identity, developing sufficient trust to allow them to execute their duties.

Computers and users in a network environment must address a similar problem. Before they can exchange information, they must be certain of each other's identity and confident that they can trust each other.

For example, a user might want to access information from a database service without compromising the integrity of his or her information. Before retrieving the information, the database service must trust the user. Likewise, users must trust a printer service before they will send it confidential information. (For example, they would not want to send private data to a phony printer service that collects confidential information and transmits it to a competitor.)

To foster the requisite trust between principals, Kerberos allows principals to identify themselves and verify their identities using secret key encryption technology. The unalterable credentials it generates allow user principals to identify themselves to network services. These credentials, called *tickets*, contain user information such as their name and location. In addition, Kerberos provides the principals with a secret key, which they use to exchange secret messages. Possession of the secret key, which allows each party to encode and decode the secret messages, constitutes verification of the credentials.

Data Integrity

An important function of computer security systems is to ensure that information is not altered or corrupted as it flows through the computer network. One solution is to encrypt all information before sending it through the network. This prevents unauthorized individuals from reading or modifying data on the network.

There are two reasons users might not want to encrypt all their data. First, not all computer networks need such a high level of security. In many cases, a security system need ensure only that data arrives at its destination unaltered. For data that falls into this category, networks might be able to use higher performance data integrity mechanisms that operate faster than data encryption.

Second, some governments impose export and import restrictions on data encryption. For example, many governments restrict the use of certain data encryption mechanisms through their public communication networks. For these reasons, users may be limited to data integrity mechanisms to protect their data.

The OSF DCE provides a high level of data integrity through the DCE RPC component. The DCE RPC ensures data integrity by using cryptographic data checksums. This allows the receiver of data to determine whether it was modified or corrupted while passing through the network.

Data checksum mechanisms take advantage of the fact that computer data is always represented in a numerical form. They employ a mathematical operation that can detect whether data has been modified.

A simple example of a data checksum is adding all the data in a single transmission and then appending the checksum onto the transmission. The receiver then could recalculate the checksum and compare it with the original. If someone on the network were to alter the data or if the data were corrupted through interference, the two checksums would differ.

Cryptographic data checksums use more complicated algorithms that make use of encryption keys to calculate the checksum. This prevents unauthorized individuals from altering the data and then updating the checksum.

Privacy of Data

The OSF DCE, through its remote procedure call (RPC) component, uses trusted *third party secret key encryption* to ensure the privacy of data. Trusted third party secret key encryption provides a method for distributing secret encryption keys to both parties of a secure communication. This method makes use of a trusted third party, called the *key distribution center* (KDC), which maintains a database of all secret keys in the distributed computing environment. Two principals may hold a secure communication by obtaining the same secret key from the KDC. This key can be used for encoding and decoding encrypted messages.

The RPC mechanism hides the complexity of the security system from the user by automatically encrypting and decrypting data as it is transferred through the network. The user need only select the level of security for each communication; the RPC does the rest of the work. A user may choose between two levels of security: private and non-private. The level determines whether all or none of the data is encrypted.

Registering Principals with DCE Registry Service

The OSF DCE registry service provides a principal registry system for creating and maintaining a database of valid principals. This distributed database system that can be accessed from any computer participating in the distributed computing environment. Like all other DCE components, the registry service is highly available, extensible, efficient, and secure.

DCE Authorization using Access Control Lists

Once users are authenticated, the service must verify which operations, such as read or modify, they are permitted to perform on the information they try to access. This process is referred to as *authorization*. A payroll office might control access to its payroll database on a per-individual basis, for example. Individuals might be allowed to look up their own salaries but not the salary of others. Financial managers might be the only ones allowed to modify salary entries.

The OSF DCE uses access control lists (ACLs) to control user access to distributed computer resources. ACLs are associated with each computer resource and contain a list of individuals and the types of operations they are permitted to perform on these resources. Examples of these operations include permission to print on a printer or modify a data record in a database.

The names in ACLs can be individual users names or names that represent a group of users. Group names are useful for providing a user access to a large number of resources. For instance, when a user joins the engineering division of a company, he or she might be given access to all engineering resources such as printers, files, and databases. Rather than adding the user's name to each resource, the administrator can add his or her name to the engineering group, thus providing the user access to all the engineering resources associated with a particular access list.

The OSF DCE access control lists are a superset of the access lists specified by the POSIX 1003.6 ACL working group. POSIX ACLs were designed to control the file access of users sharing a single computer. The extensions of DCE ACLs allow them to be useful in a distributed computing environment.

The DCE allows lists of users to have ownership and administrative rights to distributed resources. This allows more than one individual to control the types of access other users may have to these resources. In addition, the DCE allows ACLs to contain names of individuals from organizations other than the one that administers the resources the ACLs protect. For instance, a user from a company in Boston can be given individual access to a laser printer at a different company in Munich. POSIX ACLs, on the other hand, limit inclusion to members within one organization, and are applicable only to files.

Conclusion

As companies make greater use of distributed computing, the need to protect the privacy and integrity of data transmitted over networks becomes increasingly critical. The Open Software Foundation's Distributed Computing Environment addresses this need by protecting against unauthorized access to data — both intentional and inadvertent — as well as preventing the corruption of data.

The security component of DCE is fully integrated with other DCE technologies, such as the DCE RPC mechanism, to provide a high level of security without exposing the underlying complexity to application developers and end users. These features make it possible for business, engineering, and research users to work in a global computing network without compromising their private resources and confidential information. In this way the DCE provides an environment in which information can be accessed and shared securely.

D

FILE SYSTEMS
in a Distributed Computing Environment

An OSF White Paper

IN THIS CHAPTER

- OSF's Distributed File System
- Data Consistency
- Uniform File Access
- Access Security and Protection
- Reliability
- Availability
- Performance
- Manageability
- Standards Conformance
- Interoperability with NFS
- Conclusion

When personal computers started appearing, in the early 1980s, people were restricted to processing their own data locally. Not long after, the introduction of local area networks created the potential for officewide or departmental data sharing. The goal was to design a network computing environment that would make this possible.

In the mid 1980s, system vendors introduced networked file systems, which made it easy for an office of people to share information by allowing engineering workstations to export their file systems through the network. Gradually networked file systems began to grow, eventually reaching the limits of what these file systems could provide.

Today local area networks allow people to share information within an office or a department. The availability of high-performance wide area networks is making it increasingly popular to share information across the country or around the world.

Enabling people to share information worldwide requires a computing environment that allows information to flow from wherever it is stored to wherever it is needed. The challenge is to provide such an environment without exposing the complexity of the network to the end user, system administrator, or application developer. The OSF Distributed Computing Environment (DCE) meets those requirements.

OSF's Distributed File System

In 1990, the Open Software Foundation announced its selection of technologies for the Distributed Computing Environment. One of those technologies is the distributed file system (DCE DFS).

This paper provides an overview of the distributed file system component of OSF's DCE. It focuses on several key features, including data consistency, uniform access, security, reliability, availability, performance, and manageability. In addition, the paper compares the OSF distributed file system with other network file systems.

Data Consistency

Distributed file systems operate by allowing a user on a computer connected to a network to access and modify data stored in files on another computer. The computer on which the user is working is called the *client*. The computer on which the data is stored is called the *file server*.

When a user accesses data on the file server, a copy of that data is stored, or *cached*, on the client computer. Once the data is on the client, the user can read and modify it. When the user is finished modifying the data, it is written back to the file server. Problems arise when multiple users on different computers access and modify the same data. Because data from a file server is cached on the client, each user works with a different copy of the same data. Care must be taken, by the clients and servers, to ensure that each user can see changes that others are making to their copies of the data.

By allowing the file server to keep track of which clients have cached copies of the file, DCE DFS ensures that users are always working with the most recent version of their data. This tracking means that the file server keeps information, or *state*, about the clients.

DCE DFS uses a set of *tokens* to keep track of cached information. These tokens are allocated to a client by a server when the client caches data. A token is typed according to whether the client wishes to read or modify the cache entry. If a client wishes to modify a local copy of the data, it must first request a *write token* from the server, which allows the client to make the changes to the data. Because the server tracks the tokens it allocates, it can notify all other clients holding a copy of the data that their copy is no longer up to date by revoking their tokens. Those clients then must return their tokens to the server and throw away their old copies of the data.

In contrast, some existing network file systems do not keep information about which clients have copies of the data, and are therefore *stateless*. They merely specify that local data is not valid after a specified amount of time, usually a number of seconds. In other words, at any time a user could be working with data that is out of date. Stateless systems cannot adequately maintain data consistency.

Stateless file systems also have implications that go beyond data consistency. Theoretically they can recover from a system failure more easily than other systems. The server does not need to reconstruct information about the clients' states when it restarts. In addition, since a stateless server does not maintain state about its clients, it theoretically does not have a limit on how many clients it can serve. In practice, of course, this is not true.

Uniform File Access

In a distributed computing environment connecting many workstations, a user likely will have access to several different computers. For instance, a user in New York might prepare a document for a meeting in Europe using an office computer, and later amend the document from a computer in Munich. For this reason, a distributed computing environment should support global file names. One mechanism that allows the name of a file to look the same on all computers is called a *uniform name space*. Without such a mechanism, users might have difficulty finding files as they move from computer to computer and might have to return to the workstation on which they created their files to make updates efficiently.

DCE DFS solves this problem by providing an enforced uniform name space. It specifies a naming convention with which all installations must comply. DFS file access is consistent, regardless of which computer is being used or by whom. In addition, the DCE DFS naming system is designed to provide a global name space across all DFS installations. As a result, all DFS installations taken together appear as one worldwide file system.

If the file system does not provide a uniform name space, the system administrator must decide how a file server is accessed from each client. Even if administrators could maintain consistency across their administrative domain, they could not guarantee that other administrators would not configure their clients differently. Some vendors have attempted to solve this problem with a directory assistance system that distributes information about the location of various file servers. However, these systems are difficult to use, making the maintenance of a uniform name space virtually impossible.

Access Security and Protection

Distributed file systems allow individual clients easy access to many separate and distinct file servers. Their files may contain private, proprietary, or classified information. For this reason, distributed file systems must provide *authentication,* a trusted method of securely identifying the user. Once users are authenticated, the system must verify which operations they are permitted to perform on the resource they try to access. This process is referred to as *authorization*.

DCE DFS provides both the Kerberos authentication system for proving users are who they claim to be and an *access control list* mechanism for awarding access to authorized individuals.

Kerberos operates by allowing the client to exchange encrypted information with the authentication server. The encrypted message that the client receives from the server is a ticket that will allow the client access to network services such as the distributed file system. In essence, a Kerberos ticket contains information that proves a user is who he claims to be.

Access control lists allow an individual user to receive from the file server permission to perform particular operations on files or directories that are stored on a file server. For instance, a user may be given permission to read or write a file in a particular directory but be denied access to another.

Although DCE DFS is compatible with the UNIX file system, its use of access control lists provides file protection that is much stronger than that of the UNIX file system. The UNIX file system uses a simple protection mechanism to allow users access to individual files. Permissions can be awarded to either a single group of users or to all users, but cannot be awarded on a per-person basis. Although this mechanism works reasonably well on a single computer shared among a few trusted users, it does not work well in a distributed computing environment in which the number of users may extend into the thousands.

Reliability

One of the greatest advantages of a distributed file system is the elimination of the single point of failure that has dogged all time-sharing systems. The loss of a distributed network resource should not bring the entire system to a halt. However, improperly designed distributed systems introduce a new problem: a single client might rely on a number of critical resources to complete a given task. The client, in effect, cannot operate if any number of resources are unavailable. For instance, the loss of a name server, time server, authentication server, or file server could prevent a user from completing a task. To prevent this problem, a well designed distributed file system must distribute multiple copies of files or databases on multiple servers. This capability is referred to as *file* or *database replication*.

DCE DFS supports replication for all of its network services. If one of the servers becomes unavailable, a client automatically switches over to one of the replicated servers. In addition, files themselves may be replicated on multiple servers and simultaneously kept up to date. If one of the file servers becomes unavailable, a client can continue working on the replicated file copy on another server.

Most network file systems do not support replicated servers. In some cases sophisticated administrators of these file systems have created programs that automatically mount remote file systems. Unfortunately this only works if the file systems happen to be available at the time the system starts running. In addition, this type of service is difficult to set up and does not allow the client to switch to another server if the currently mounted server crashes.

Availability

Ideally, the components of a distributed file system should be available to users at all times. A well designed system, such as DCE DFS, allows system administrators to perform routine maintenance of the servers' hardware, software, and data while the file server is in operation and available to users. Typical administrative activities include moving of disk data across file servers, file backups, and checking file system consistency after a server crashes.

Other network file systems are not designed to provide this high level of availability. Most of them use the standard UNIX file system, which is unavailable to users during much of the system administration.

Many of the features that make DCE DFS reliable also enable it to be highly available to users. For instance, use of replication enables an administrator to do file system backups while the system is up and running. Normally, performing a backup on a file while it is being modified could result in a corrupted backup version of the file. DFS avoids this problem by creating a replicated copy of the file system, then backing up the copy. The net effect is that the replicated copy remains stable even while the user is changing the original file.

In contrast, a standard UNIX file system must be taken off line before an administrator can back it up. The typical method of backing up most network file servers is first to schedule server down time, take the server down so that only the administrator can use it, and finally start file system backups. During a backup, which may take a significant amount of time, the system is unavailable to users. When the backup is complete, the server is once again available to users.

Another feature that increases the availability of a server is the ability to move files between disks without taking the server out of service. Often an administrator is faced with one disk that is filled to capacity while another is empty. The administrator must shuffle files from one disk to another to provide users the disk space they need to continue their work.

DCE DFS allows administration to move files from one disk to another while the system is available. This flexibility is possible because the name of a file is independent of its physical location. This feature is referred to as *location transparency*.

In network file systems that do not support location transparency, users can see their files move from one partition to another because their file names change with the move. As a result, a user must stop working while the file move is taking place. If the user has a program that explicitly knows about the location of these files, it must be changed, or at least restarted.

A highly available distributed file system must be able to recover quickly from system failures. After a system crash, many file systems, such as the UNIX file system, must go through a check phase to ensure that the file system structure was not corrupted. Corruption can occur because many of today's fast file systems keep much of the housekeeping information about the file system, such as unallocated disk areas, in main memory, and only update it to disk every 30 seconds. A chance exists for the server to crash before this information is updated to disk. In most cases, this information can be reconstructed during the check phase. Unfortunately, the check phase can take a long time.

DCE DFS uses a file system that keeps a log of every disk operation that occurs between updates of this housekeeping information. If the server crashes, only changes made to the disk since the last update are checked and reconstructed. This greatly reduces the file system check phase and allows quick file server restarts. These *log-based file systems* are derived from transaction logging systems that have been a popular means of maintaining data integrity in relational databases.

In contrast, non-log-based file systems, such as the UNIX file system, must run a file system check after a server restart. During this time, the server is unavailable to users. For a large file system containing many gigabytes of data, this translates to a significant amount of additional down-time.

Performance

Another advantage of a distributed file system is the ability to share information with many diverse users. The ideal would be one worldwide file system that would allow global information sharing. Such a system would have to scale well and work very efficiently; otherwise it might overwhelm the available computer and network resources.

DCE DFS is an efficient, extensible system. Unlike other file systems, DCE DFS caches on the client computer large amounts of information on file status as well as data. This means that the client makes fewer data requests from the file server, thus reducing server and network load. In addition, the server tracks which clients have cached copies of files, reducing the need for the client to constantly query the server, as well as reducing the network and server load.

Network file systems that allow the client to cache only a small amount of data and do not have mechanisms for ensuring that the cached information is up to date must communicate frequently with the file server. These systems use up much of the available network and file server resources.

Manageability

As mentioned above, a distributed file system should use as little of the computer and network resources as possible. In addition, this file system also should be easy to manage.

DCE DFS makes use of distributed databases to keep track of file location, authentication, and access control lists used by the file servers and clients. These databases are broken into domains that are separately administered and maintained, but can be accessed by any client. In addition, these databases are self-configuring and easy to operate.

Managing a network file system that does not use distributed databases to keep track of configuration information, such as the location of files, is difficult because this information must be stored on the individual file servers and clients computers. To manage such a system, an administrator must connect to each client and file server and make changes to this configuration information.

Standards Conformance

DCE DFS conforms with the IEEE POSIX 1003.1 file system semantics standard. Such conformance is important because this standard allows applications to be portable across many hardware and software platforms.

Interoperability with NFS

The distributed file system component of OSF's Distributed Computing Environment provides protocol gateways that allow clients using Network File System (NFS) clients to interoperate with DCE DFS file servers. These gateways provide a migration path to DCE DFS for those sites already dependent on NFS. In addition, the gateways allow NFS clients to access the uniform name space provided by DCE DFS.

Conclusion

Today's computing environment is dramatically different from the computing environment of a few years ago. The availability of personal computers, local area networks, and high-performance wide area networks is creating the potential for worldwide information sharing.

OSF's integrated Distributed Computing Environment, via its distributed file system, goes beyond today's networked file systems. For example, its use of the token manager ensures shared data consistency across multiple clients. Moreover, its design enforces a uniform name space. DCE DFS uses Kerberos authentication and provides authorization through the use of access control lists. In addition, DCE DFS allows its databases and files to be replicated, which provides for reliability and availability. Because it uses remotely managed databases to provide all of its services, DCE DFS also is easy to manage. Furthermore, it can interoperate with NFS clients through the use of protocol gateways.

OSF's distributed file system meets the needs of today's information-intensive environments by enabling people to reliably and easily access data wherever it is stored and use it wherever it is needed.

E

THE OSF

Distributed Management Environment

An OSF White Paper

IN THIS CHAPTER

- Selection Through an Open Process
- OSF and Interoperability
- The Benefits of a Distributed Management Environment
- Components of the Distributed Management Environment
- A Program Update and Timetable
- DME Evaluation Team

The advent of the open systems movement is changing the way people think about computers and computer networks. Until recently, proprietary systems predominated, and systems administrators took for granted the sophisticated management facilities those systems provide. PC users did not rely on support from systems administrators; they could perform many simple maintenance tasks themselves.

As organizations assembled multi-vendor environments, system management changed. Today, system administrators and users can no longer count on their familiarity with a few administrative approaches to maintain a diverse computing environment. Instead, they must contend with inconsistent management schemes resulting from the lack of a common approach based on standards.

The task of managing stand-alone systems from multiple vendors as well as a growing number of distributed systems has led to unpredictable and complicated system management procedures that result in costly training and other expenditures.

The Open Software Foundation (OSF) is addressing this critical problem. Using its Request for Technology (RFT) process, OSF has solicited from the worldwide computer industry proposals that define and implement a distributed management environment (DME). The DME technology that OSF selects will strive to fulfill the open systems promise of a unified approach for efficiently managing systems, networks, and user applications. It will provide a framework that supports a consistent administrative approach as well as applications for managing distributed systems. The DME selection will simplify the problem of managing distributed systems and reduce the costs of system administration for organizations worldwide.

Selection Through an Open Process

OSF is in a singular position to implement such a distributed management environment. Its charter is to make available an open, portable software environment, selecting and implementing the industry's best technologies in an unbiased manner. OSF membership is made up of computer hardware and software suppliers, end users, educational institutions, government agencies, and other interested organizations.

OSF uses an innovative open process to provide a level playing field on which every submitter of technology is provided an equal opportunity to participate. This open process rests on four cornerstones.

Membership Special-Interest Groups (SIGs). Made up of experts from member companies, SIGs have a powerful voice in the open process. They help define the scope and requirements for RFTs and suggest preliminary evaluation criteria.

Open Technology Acquisition. In evaluating technology for its open computing environment, OSF receives input from many sources. Through the RFT process, OSF solicits and evaluates proposals from the computer industry, research institutions, government agencies, and end users. All OSF members, submitters of technology, and other interested parties are invited to contribute ideas on technological and market needs and recommend evaluation criteria. Relevant standards organizations and consortia contribute to the technology evaluation as well. At review meetings, nonmembers who have submitted proposals and nonmember representatives from relevant standards bodies and consortia can provide the same level of input as OSF members. Taking into consideration the recommendations of its membership and industry consultants, OSF will select technology for its Distributed Management Environment offering.

Member Meetings. On a regular basis, OSF meets with its membership to exchange ideas on open systems technology. In addition, members review proposals submitted through the RFT process and provide input to OSF's evaluation teams.

Equal and Timely Access to Technologies under Review and Development. OSF's RFT and development processes provide members with timely access to open systems technologies. Through previews of code in development, called snapshots, members can evaluate the software, develop their own applications in parallel with the efforts of OSF, and port the software to their systems. OSF's snapshot program thus ensures rapid transfer of technology to the industry.

OSF and Interoperability

Through an earlier RFT, OSF solicited technologies for distributed computing technologies. The result, the OSF Distributed Computing Environment (DCE), took the computer industry beyond connectivity to a new level of interoperability among diverse systems.

The DCE is an integrated software environment that makes a network of systems from a variety of vendors appear as a consistent, unified system. By masking the technical complexities of the network, the DCE provides users transparent access to diverse network resources. With DCE, users can access information and applications freely from anywhere in the network, while protecting data from unauthorized access through effective security.

The DCE has been endorsed enthusiastically by the computer industry as an important step toward bridging open and proprietary systems in a multi-vendor network.

With the DCE as a solid foundation, OSF is continuing to provide additional interoperability to its open computing environment. A poll of OSF members in early 1990 indicated that an overriding majority wanted OSF to address distributed management as its next major effort in the area of interoperability.

The Benefits of a Distributed Management Environment

A distributed management environment allows a heterogeneous computing network to be managed in a uniform and efficient manner through a consistent user interface. Taking advantage of a distributed management environment, computer users will be able to concentrate on their applications and spend less time and effort managing their systems.

The distributed management environment that OSF offers will provide many benefits for end users, applications developers, and vendors of systems and software.

For the end user or system administrator, a distributed management environment will

1. Provide consistent appearance and behavior for management applications

2. Improve the reliability and availability of systems and networks

3. Increase the portability of user skills between different platforms

4. Reduce the skill level required to perform management tasks

5. Reduce the time, training, and associated costs required to perform management tasks

6. Provide the ability for centralized as well as distributed management of systems

For software vendors, a distributed management environment will

1. Provide a framework for the development of portable management applications, comparable in sophistication to those found in proprietary systems

2. Provide support for a common appearance and behavior among management applications

3. Provide the development environment for management applications that manage both stand-alone and distributed systems.

4. Create an expanded market for management applications

5. Provide an opportunity for ISVs to make their software packages portable to various management environments (for example, packages that monitor traffic on a network).

For system vendors, the distributed management environment will

1. Provide a framework that facilitates the development and integration of new as well as upgraded management technologies

2. Provide an open systems management environment for multi-vendor systems and networks

3. Reduce development and maintenance costs associated with system management applications.

The DME will implement appropriate standards and establish the basis for the evolution of future specifications and standards by providing the best technologies available.

Components of the Distributed Management Environment

A major objective of the DME RFT is to identify a *common framework* for managing networked systems. This framework will support the consistent management of a wide range of systems, from stand-alone systems to those in a distributed environment. OSF's high standards for extensibility, maintainability and adaptability require such a common framework, supported by appropriate management tools.

The following diagram outlines the components of the DME model, as specified in the DME RFT.

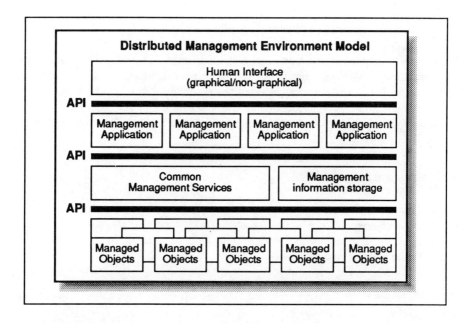

The DME framework will define *application programming interfaces* (APIs) that applications use to invoke common management services, store and retrieve management information, and exchange management information with managed objects in local and remote systems.

User Interface

The *user interface* for management applications will support both a character cell (nongraphical) and a graphical interface. It will be easy to use and will perform consistently for all management applications.

Management Applications

Management applications perform management tasks, such as remote reinitialization of network nodes and remote reconfiguration of parameters of network nodes, by communicating with and manipulating representations of computing resources, called *managed objects*. The distributed management environment will include applications that provide the basic means to manage any open system, from a single system to a large, heterogeneous network of systems. These management applications shield the user from the detailed procedures necessary to perform management tasks.

Common Management Services

Common management services support the management framework by providing programming interfaces used by management applications. These services include such functionality as management communications, event management and logging, and object management. They enable the development of portable management applications and allow interoperability between heterogeneous systems.

Management Information Storage Services

Management information storage services allow management applications to store and retrieve information in a uniform manner. These services will be presented through a common programming interface that is independent of the underlying storage mechanisms.

Managed Objects

A *managed object* is a representation of a computing resource or any other conceptual entity within the computing environment. An example of a system resource is a file system, which is represented and managed through one or more associated managed objects. Other examples include devices, print and mail systems, users, and end-user application software. To make management applications portable, extensible, and adaptable, a general interface to the managed objects is required. Intrinsic functionality to support managed objects will be provided.

A Program Update and Timetable

OSF issued the Distributed Management Environment RFT on July 31, 1990. It distributed 5000 copies of the RFT, announced it in academic and trade publications, and posted it on numerous electronic bulletin boards, and the *submission phase* of the RFT began. By September 21, OSF had received 42 letters of intent to submit technology.

In early October 1990, OSF hosted a meeting of technology submitters, Management SIG members, the DME evaluation team and consultants, and relevant standards body representatives to review the initial evaluation criteria recommended by the OSF Management Special Interest Group (SIG). This meeting established equal opportunity for all participants in the DME RFT by making these criteria and copies of the technology summaries available to all the groups represented.

At the November OSF Member Meeting, in a dedicated DME Track, each submitting company was given the opportunity to present its technology to OSF membership. More than 250 people participated in the four days of review that included four panel discussions, 34 presentations by submitting companies, and informal discussions. Participants returned to their companies with questionnaires that were due back to OSF by January 18, 1991.

The deadline for full submissions to OSF was December 15, 1990. The following is a list of submitters to the DME RFT.

Bolt, Berenek, Newman Communications Corporation

British Telecom

Dialogue Switching Technologies USA, Inc.

Digital Equipment Corporation

DSET Corp.

Fraunhofer Gesellschaft

Gradient Technologies

Groupe Bull

Hewlett-Packard Company

IBM Corp.

Legato Systems, Inc.

Massachusetts Institute of Technology (Project Athena)

Microsoft

NCR (Network Products Division)

NeXT Computer, Inc.

Quality Software Products

Quantum Gesellschaft fuer Software GmbH

Sceptre Corp.

Siemens Nixdorf Informationsysteme

Stollmann GmbH

Systar

Tivoli Systems, Inc.

Touch Communications, Inc.

UniSolutions Associates

Wang Laboratories

Distributed Management Environment RFT Schedule		
Submission	**Evaluation**	**Selection**
1990	**1991**	
Jul Aug Sep Oct Nov Dec	Jan Feb Mar Apr May	Jun Jul Aug Sep Oct Nov

As the timeline indicates, the *evaluation phase* continues through March 1991, when submitters and OSF members meet with OSF's Distributed Management Environment Evaluation Team to provide final input to the RFT. Subsequently, a laboratory evaluation period will allow selected submitters to demonstrate their technologies under laboratory conditions. After assessing the scope, quality, and completeness of those submissions, OSF will move to the *selection phase* of the project. Announcement of the distributed management environment technology is planned for the second half of 1991.

DME Evaluation Team

The DME evaluation team is composed of experts in distributed management from around the world. It includes full-time OSF development staff and highly qualified consultants from industry, academia, and the standards community who specialize in various areas of distributed management technology.

DME Consultants

R. Scott Butler E. I. DuPont Information Systems

Martin Kirk X/Open; Chairman of IEEE POSIX 1003.7

Professor Lindsay Marshall University of Newcastle upon Tyne

George Mouradian AT&T Bell Labs

Bruce Murrill Network Management Forum

David Passmore Ernst & Young

Karsten Prey Diebold Deutschland

Phil Shevrin Locus Computing Corporation

Daniel Stokesberry National Institute of Standards Technology

Hans Strack-Zimmermann iXos Computer GmbH

DME Evaluation Team

Dr. Matthias Autrata
Dr. Andras Balazs
Kathryn Birkbeck
Daniel Geer
Jonathan Gossels
Steve Knight
Norbert Marrek
Dr. Franco Miralles
Michael Santifaller
Arno Schmidt
Hartmut Streppel

The following paper was written by OSF in January, 1991. We do not publish it here as an attempt at independent and impartial analysis, but rather as part of the effort—given substance throughout this entire book—to make widely available the official claims and specifications regarding the OSF/1 operating system.

Realizing, however, that the following OSF document is highly tendentious, we sought permission to publish a similar comparison—but one written from a contrary point of view—by UNIX International on behalf of System V, Release 4. UI denied us this permission. However, we suggest that you obtain the UI paper by writing or calling

UNIX International
20 Waterview Boulevard
Parsippany, New Jersey 07054
Tel. 1-800-848-6495

Then make some comparisons of your own.

—eds.

AN ANALYSIS:

OSF/1 and System V, Release 4

An OSF White Paper

Table of Contents

Notice to Readers

While every attempt has been made to ensure the accuracy of all the information in this document, OSF assumes no liability to any party for loss or damage, whether direct, indirect, incidental, or consequential, caused by errors or omissions or by statements of any kind in this document, or for the use of any product or system described herein. The reader shall bear the sole responsibility for his/her actions taken in reliance on the information in this document.

This document may be freely copied and distributed in whole or in part, provided the user includes in any such copy, OSF's copyright notice, and a conspicuously worded statement that the copies have been made with the permission of the copyright owner, Open Software Foundation, Inc.

Executive Summary

Both the OSF/1 operating system, from the Open Software Foundation, and UNIX System V Release 4 (SVR4) provide the compatibility, portability, scalability, and interoperability features required as a base for open systems computing environments. Both systems are available now and both systems have access to thousands of applications written for standards-based systems.

What sets OSF/1 apart from SVR4, for users charged with making operating system choices for their businesses, are the innovative features of the OSF/1 operating system. These features provide the benefits of higher performance, greater security, and increased data availability in a more flexible operating system.

Symmetric multiprocessing, enhanced security, logical volume management, flexible program management, a simplified system architecture, and a clear growth path to modular, microkernel-based systems, enable OSF/1 to satisfy the requirements of today while forming a base for the next generation of open systems. These features, along with standards-based interfaces, will support businesses well into the future.

Introduction

The choice of an operating system for a company's business — whether for a system vendor, independent software vendor (ISV), or an end user — is an important one. This choice determines not only the capabilities of current systems, but also how readily one can take advantage of new developments in technology without losing investments in current software applications.

This choice becomes even more important as vendors and users move into the era of open systems. In an open systems environment, users can mix and match hardware from various vendors to best meet their needs, and software must be portable and interoperable among all these machines. Such an environment places special demands on its operating systems.

Operating systems for open computing environments must adhere to industrywide standards and specifications for the interfaces they provide to system and applications software. These interfaces are one enabler of the open systems goal of application portability. The operating system itself must be portable enough to be moved easily onto different classes of hardware — from personal computers to supercomputers — to enable users to increase processing power as their business needs grow, without the need to rewrite applications. This is the open systems goal of scalability. In the diverse environment of open systems, each system must communicate and cooperate easily with its neighbors and associates whether they are in the same room or on the other side of the world. This is the open systems goal of interoperability.

The open systems environment is an idea whose time has arrived. It brings the benefits of economy, performance, protection of investments, and freedom to users formerly locked in to relationships with a single vendor and their product lines. These benefits can only be realized by operating system software that is as innovative in concept and as ambitious in scope as the idea of open systems itself. The OSF/1 operating system is such software.

This paper examines the OSF/1 operating system and the UNIX System V Release 4 operating system from UNIX System Laboratories (USL). Both the OSF/1 operating system and UNIX System V Release 4 meet the basic open system requirements for portability, scalability, and interoperability. But only the OSF/1 operating system goes beyond today's requirements to provide benefits for users implementing open systems for the 1990s and into the next century.

These benefits include

- The ability to increase a system's performance cost-effectively through the use of multiprocessing hardware

- The protection of sensitive data and installations through enhanced security functionality

- The availability of critical data whenever it is needed through commercial processing capabilities such as logical volume management and disk mirroring

- Increased system flexibility through the ability to reconfigure the system while it is running

- A redesigned operating system core that reduces the costs associated with system maintenance and modification and provides a clear path for future growth.

A detailed feature by feature comparison of OSF/1 and UNIX System V Release 4 is included in the appendices for easy reference. The remainder of this document will clearly indicate the technical superiority of OSF/1, why it is the right technological base for the next generation of open systems, and why choosing it makes business sense for organizations on an open systems path.

Innovation

Mach

The OSF/1 operating system brings users the benefits of technological advances in operating system design and function while protecting investments in current software and systems. Mach kernel technology from Carnegie Mellon University, at the core of OSF/1, has been developed and refined over the last six years under the auspices of the U.S. Defense Advanced Research Project Agency (DARPA) with contributions from other industrial research and commercial organizations. Today, thousands of Mach-based systems have been shipped by commercial suppliers including Encore Computer Corporation, NeXT, Inc., Sequent Computer Corporation, and others. Other vendors, including Digital Equipment Corporation, Hewlett-Packard, Hitachi, IBM, and Intergraph have begun the move to Mach-based OSF/1 systems with shipments beginning in 1991.

Mach technology provides the OSF/1 system with integral support for multiprocessor hardware. The fully symmetric multiprocessing capabilities of OSF/1 enables users to achieve maximum performance from multiprocessor hardware and applications written for multiprocessing.

For users investing now in open systems solutions, support for multiprocessing is crucial. Multiprocessor machines provide the next level of price/performance and power benefits to users as chip densities and cycle times become more difficult to improve. Users needing increased computing capacity will find that adding processors to their existing multiprocessing hardware is significantly more economical than the alternative of replacing their entire computer system. Investments in operating systems that do not provide multiprocessing support will put users at a competitive disadvantage.

Mach technology also provides the OSF/1 system with an integrated threads facility. By allowing separate pieces of applications to execute simultaneously, threads bring to applications and their users the benefits of increased application performance (on multiprocessor hardware) and more cleanly structured applications for lowered maintenance costs. In uniprocessor environments the use of threads may increase performance by the overlapping of execution and I/O threads.

The OSF/1 kernel also is threaded so that kernel processes can execute simultaneously on a multiprocessor system for the highest systemwide performance. Traditional UNIX systems, such as System V Release 4, do not utilize threads, either in applications or in the kernel. These systems, even when modified for multiprocessing, face the same performance constraints as non-multiprocessing operating systems because kernel processes must execute sequentially on a single processor.

Architecture

The OSF/1 system provides a simplified system architecture compared to traditional UNIX systems. The Mach core of the OSF/1 system provides basic operating system services and is highly portable to different computer architectures due to a clean separation of machine-dependent and machine-independent code. This type of code separation is carried on throughout most of the OSF/1 system modules. Other operating system services are layered on the Mach core in a modular fashion to provide the remainder of UNIX services.

This innovative architecture will enable OSF, as part of its long-range strategy for the OSF/1 operating system, to move many services traditionally part of UNIX kernels out of the OSF/1 kernel into user space. This will leave a smaller, cleaner kernel requiring fewer transitions to supervisor mode to get work done. What will be left is the OSF/1 microkernel, or "pure" kernel, providing basic system services, with modular "server" processes, such as networking or file system servers, layered above it. The servers will be cleanly separated from the kernel with specifications for the interface between kernel and servers made freely available to the industry. The OSF/1 system has already begun this process by providing a program loader that operates in user space.

Security

The innovative security technology within OSF/1 enables users to protect sensitive data and installations against unauthorized use and virus attack. It provides the best base for developing today's trusted applications for both government and commercial users. The OSF/1 security features are integral to the operating system rather than added on. Since security is designed in, it is complementary with the remainder of the operating system functionality. In particular, it provides security in a multiprocessing environment in a seamless way. SVR4 on the other hand is adding on either multiprocessing or security to an existing release, keeping users waiting for a fully integrated mix of these features. The implications of this "after the fact" approach are obvious. OSF/1 provides an alternative — multiprocessing and security features that are an integral part of the overall system design.

Enhanced Data Availability

To provide additional commercial-quality functionality, OSF/1 includes an innovative logical volume manager (LVM). The LVM increases system reliability and performance by transparently creating mirror images of files on different physical storage devices. For applications that create large files, such as database management systems, the LVM removes the traditional UNIX system limitation that restricts files to a single physical volume (for example, a disk pack). With the OSF/1 logical volume manager, files and file systems can span multiple physical volumes. This functionality is based on technology supplied to OSF by IBM, a leader in commercially oriented products.

Conclusion

OSF's approach to operating system architecture has resulted in a coherent, open, sensible, modular tool with the features required for commercial open systems included by design — not tacked on as is the case with traditional UNIX operating systems. OSF/1 provides today's implementors of open systems with the immediate benefits of increased performance through symmetric multiprocessing, enhanced security, and high data and system availability in a commercial-quality, standards-compliant operating system. It also provides users with peace of mind via compatibility with current applications and a clear future growth path.

System V Release 4 does not provide similar innovations. The current UNIX International "road map," a requirements document for System V development, calls for availability of integrated multiprocessing and security features some time in 1992. UI/USL would prefer to down play these fundamental architectural issues and concentrate on discrete feature by feature comparisons. But while the specific lower level features of both systems (described later in this paper) are basically similar, the integral architecture of OSF/1 as described above is *the major differentiator* between the two systems. Its significance should not be lost on those evaluating the two.

Innovation via the Open Process

The operating system is only one component of a complete open systems environment. Additional layered technology, such as the graphical user interface and distributed computing environment, is required to provide a total open systems solution. This technology is provided via the Open Software Foundation's open process. It is through this process, open to the worldwide information technology industry, that OSF determines the needs of its members — including systems vendors, software developers, end users, and academic and research organizations

— and obtains the best technology to meet these needs. OSF members can influence the technical direction of the OSF/1 operating system to best suit their needs. This influence is expressed through OSF/1 Special Interest Group meetings, general member interaction with OSF staff, and through the OSF Portability Lab, where member company engineers work alongside OSF staff while porting OSF technology to their own platforms. The give-and-take of the Portability Lab resulted in OSF/1 code which was exceptionally clean and free of hardware-specific idiosyncrasies upon its first release.

Layered technology for the OSF/1 operating system includes the OSF/Motif graphical user interface and OSF's Distributed Computing Environment (DCE), which provides operating system and network-independent distributed computing services. Motif has become the dominant graphical user interface for open systems and the recently announced DCE technologies already have been widely accepted by the computer industry.

Through its open process and Requests for Technology (RFT), OSF will continue to provide leading-edge enabling technology for a complete, portable, scalable, interoperable open systems environment. Selections of technology for an Architecture-Neutral software Distribution Format (ANDF) will be finalized in the second quarter of 1991. ANDF will create a single market for mass-market open systems software by enabling developers to produce and package one version of their product for all the systems found in this diverse environment. The recent RFT for a distributed management environment (DME) will provide a management framework and tools for system management in an open systems distributed environment. The selection of technology to comprise DME will be announced in Q3 1991.

Base Operating System Functionality

Kernel

The OSF/1 kernel's compact, modular Mach component provides the basic services of scheduling, memory management, and interprocess communication. Subsystems are layered on top of the Mach component in a modular way to provide other system services, such as managing the file-system. The result is an easier to understand, flexible, more manageable and more portable system than other UNIX implementations.

Over time, traditional UNIX systems have suffered from the accretion of new features into the operating system kernel. What started as a relatively small and compact operating system has grown progressively larger. Today's UNIX systems are large, complex and difficult to maintain. The OSF/1 system with its Mach foundation represents the first step in a return to the original concept of a small and compact operating system. OSF/1's architecture today is an integration of the Berkeley Software Distribution (BSD) UNIX kernel functionality with the Mach functionality, enhanced by security, multiprocessing, streams and other features. Although integrated, there is a cleanly defined interface between the UNIX portion and the Mach portion allowing for an orderly separation in a future release. This architecture will support the future migration of many UNIX kernel services into user space, thereby enhancing maintainability, extensibility, and flexibility and giving the software developer more control over the use of its facilities.

From their presentations, it appears that USL has done some work to make SVR4 more modular than SVR3, probably as part of their goal of achieving a B2 security evaluation from the National Computer Security Center in a later release (see section on security). The UI road map implies that System V will be redesigned sometime in the future. This redesign is sometimes referred to as "System V.5". However, the road map gives no solid evidence when this may take place.

Multiprocessing

Driven by ever lower costs per central processing unit (CPU), multiprocessing is becoming an indispensable tool for improving the performance of computer systems. Because applications spend a significant portion of their time using kernel services, a kernel specifically designed for multiprocessing is important for overall system throughput. The Mach kernel at the core of OSF/1 was designed from the outset for multiprocessing.

OSF/1 provides fully symmetric multiprocessing, or SMP, the multiprocessing approach that for most applications yields the highest performance. SMP ensures that all processing tasks are divided as evenly as possible across all the processors in a system. This eliminates the bottlenecks that can hurt application performance in asymmetric multiprocessing systems. SMP ensures that multiprocessing hardware is used to its utmost efficiency.

OSF/1's symmetric multiprocessing support is integral to the design of the OSF/1 Mach kernel. In conjunction with Encore Computer Corporation, OSF has parallelized the OSF/1 subsystems to enhance system performance, including general system calls; the NFS-compatible, UFS, and VFS file systems; the virtual-memory subsystem; the TCP/IP/UDP/ARP protocol suites; the STREAMS framework; and the BSD sockets framework. Subsystem parallelization, which is lacking on SVR4, significantly enhances multiprocessor performance.

OSF/1 takes full advantage of multiprocessing machines while ensuring continued compatibility with uniprocessor machines. To provide backward compatibility with unparallelized kernel subsystems, OSF/1 employs a unique funnel mechanism, which provides a transition from parallelized to unparallelized layers.

Because fully symmetric multiprocessing is an integral part of the basic operating system design, the feature is present in all OSF/1 configurations. It does not restrict the availability of other sophisticated technology, such as the B1-certifiable set of security features.

SVR4 does not support multiprocessing. USL has announced its plans to add multiprocessing on top of the SVR4 foundation, but in a somewhat complicated two-phase implementation. The first release of Standard Symmetrical Multiprocessing, called SVR4 MP, is expected in 1H91 and will be done in partnership with Intel, Motorola, NCR, OKI, Olivetti, and Unisys.

Also during 1H91, USL is planning to release its enhanced security version of SVR4 called SVR4 ES. It is important to note that SVR4 ES is an entirely different source code base than SVR4 MP. Both bases have a common origin from SVR4 but will be totally separate releases. A user must either choose security or choose multiprocessing, since they will not be available in the same release.

The release of a fully symmetric multiprocessing version will have to wait until at least 1992. This release, merged with the security version, will be called SVR4 ES/MP. The primary partner is Sequent with help from Pyramid, Fujitsu, Motorola, and ICL. Details of what the "standard" symmetric MP will include and how it will differ from the "fully" symmetric MP are not clear at this time.

It is expected that vendors will have significant work to do to move from SVR4 to SVR4 MP or to SVR4 ES and then again to go to SVR4 ES/MP. It is obvious that the SVR4 ES/MP release, which combines security and multiprocessing, is the release more resembling OSF/1 in functionality, and its 1992 release date clearly puts USL about two years behind OSF/1 in the delivery of integrated functionality. The 1H91 Standard MP is obviously an attempt to provide a quick response to OSF/1. Because of the amount of work required to port to the SVR4 MP release and then again to the SVR4 ES/MP release a year later (and the effect this will have on the user base) it is not clear how many vendors will use the SVR4 MP release.

Threads

OSF/1's kernel includes a threads facility, which permits multiple threads to share address space, file descriptors, and so on, thereby allowing multiple instruction streams to run concurrently within a single process memory space. This threads facility provides support for application level threads through a POSIX 1003.4a compliant programming interface. Threads allow application developers to write applications which essentially have cooperating routines all sharing access to the same data in memory. In an OSF/1 system, these threads can execute on any available processor in a multiprocessor system, thereby taking advantage of the power of multiprocessing hardware. Using threads, instead of traditional UNIX facilities, allows developers to provide easier and more natural solutions for many types of problems, especially those handling multiple asynchronous events. Developers can write applications so that each thread has a small self-contained job. Each thread, operating independently of other threads could process one request for service and respond at a higher rate than a traditional UNIX application using multiple processes. A multi-threaded program, even though originally written on a uniprocessor, can automatically, without modification, take advantage of additional processors in a multiprocessor system. Even on a uniprocessor system, threads can improve performance by providing an easy way to overlap computation and input/output.

SVR4 does not offer a threads facility. UI is on record as saying that threads is not an important method for improving performance. It should be noted that the IEEE thinks enough about the value of threads, and that they will be commonly used, to want to standardize their usage with the emerging POSIX 1003.4a draft standard. We believe that threads will become a major programming paradigm in the 1990s.

Security

The proliferation of open computer environments is a boon to productivity, but with this comes a potential security threat. The OSF/1 operating system has powerful security features oriented toward access control and system auditing, and provides state-of-the-art system administrative controls to ensure the system integrity that is required in today's computer environments.

OSF/1's security technology is targeted for evaluation at the B1 level of trust (as defined by the U.S. National Computer Security Center's Trusted Computer Security Evaluation Criteria), but also includes many B2 and B3 features such as least privilege, trusted facility management, and access control lists. The OSF/1 security functionality has been implemented in a modular fashion to allow system vendors maximum flexibility in configuring security features when building the system.

The OSF/1 operating system can be configured with standard UNIX, C2, or B1 level security. All of the security features are provided as modules and are conditionally included in the system at compile time. This allows the system vendor to work with one source code base, thereby avoiding the expense associated with maintaining both a standard and a trusted system. Since there is a common base this also ensures that the security-enhanced kernel functionality remains completely compatible with the standard kernel functionality even as the system evolves through new releases.

SecureWare Inc, the leading supplier of security technology for UNIX systems, was selected by OSF to provide the security for the OSF/1 operating system. In choosing SecureWare's technology, OSF has not only endorsed a proven solution, but is taking advantage of SecureWare's TAPI (Trusted Application Programming Interface), which is already widely adopted in the industry. Trusted applications compatible with TAPI can be readily ported to OSF/1 systems. This gives OSF/1 vendors and customers a head start in trusted systems.

USL offers similar security features in its Multi-Level Security product, but this is provided on a System V Release 3.2 base and is not compatible with SVR4. USL plans to add B2-level security features to an upcoming version of SVR4 (SVR4 ES) in 1991.

OSF/1, through its planned evolution to a microkernel base, provides an architectural path to B3 certification. SVR4's large, monolithic kernel will preclude its evaluation at the B3 level. B3-level security, because of the requirement for a small, compact trusted computing base, cannot be provided in SVR4 until the System V kernel is substantially redesigned.

Memory Management

Virtual Memory Management

OSF/1 includes all machine-dependent portions of the memory management subsystem in one clearly defined and easy-to-port module. All other portions of the subsystem are machine independent and need not be changed when porting OSF/1 to a new architecture.

OSF/1 provides the Mach advanced virtual-memory management system, which manages the utilization of system memory resources and ensures that concurrently executing programs share memory effectively.

OSF/1 supports page-level operations and lets processes access files and devices as ranges of bytes within the virtual address space of the process. In addition, it enables programs to access and share data while maintaining data consistency. The virtual-memory mechanisms of OSF/1 allow libraries and other code to be shared among processes. OSF/1 also uses copy-on-write optimizations to speed up process spawning and the passing of large amounts of data between processes.

SVR4's capabilities, although not based on Mach technology, are similar in this area. The Mach technology provides a foundation for additional virtual memory capabilities not present in SVR4.

External Memory Management

The OSF/1 kernel provides an external memory-management interface that allows tasks — called external pagers — to extend the virtual memory paging operations provided by the OSF/1 kernel. An external pager is a user space task which cooperates with the kernel to manage the way data is moved between main memory and external storage. An external pager creates a memory object representing the data to be managed. Requests for that data by application programs and the operating system kernel are handled by the memory object's pager. External pagers are especially useful for applications that must maintain fine control of memory management, such as distributed transaction processing systems.

SVR4 does not support external pagers.

File Systems

OSF/1's file system architecture, based on the Berkeley 4.4 Virtual File System (VFS), is modular, providing clean, well-defined interfaces within the kernel. Several file systems are supported for compatibility and interoperability with existing UNIX systems. The OSF/1 environment provides support for the following file systems

• 4.3 BSD Tahoe Fast File System

• An NFS-compatible network file system

• A System V file system.

The NFS-compatible file system and the 4.3BSD file system have been parallelized to take advantage of OSF/1's inherent multiprocessing capabilities. Applications utilizing these file systems on multiprocessing hardware will experience increased performance.

Both OSF/1 and SVR4 implement a virtual file system architecture similar to the VFS/vnode interface, which enables multiple file-system types to be used transparently. The Virtual File System is an abstraction layered above the individual file systems. The VFS can connect UFS, NFS, and other file-system types.

SVR4 provides a 4.3BSD, a System V file system, and Sun's NFS. SVR4 provides four additional file systems:

• RFS

• /proc

• Fifo file system

• Spec file system

Functionality similar to that provided by /proc and FIFO file systems is provided in OSF/1. The /proc file system provides a mechanism for the owner of a process to look at the process' address space. OSF/1 provides similar functionality via the ptrace facility. Specific capabilities provided by /proc not currently in ptrace may be added in the future, if this becomes a market requirement. FIFOs in OSF/1 are implemented as part of all the file systems rather than as a separate file system.

SVR4 RFS is a functional subset of the OSF Distributed Computing Environment (DCE) AFS file system. Users wishing full distributed support can license DCE technology separately from OSF.

Internationalization

OSF/1 provides XPG3 base features and in addition includes multibyte character support. Locale databases (collections of facts about a specific country or culture) and message catalogs (allowing translation of user messages without altering the source code) are supported. The commands within OSF/1 also have been internationalized.

To support European languages, OSF/1 provides the XPG3 mechanisms, including eight-bit clean commands and localization capabilities. For the Asian market, OSF/1 provides Shift JIS encoding and an enhanced tty driver to provide input capabilities for Japanese.

USL's MNLS package, which offers similar internationalization capabilities as OSF/1, is currently available as a separate release for the SVR4 base. This functionality is expected to be integrated with the mainline SVR4 release in mid-1991. Both SVR4 and OSF/1 will track and implement the XPG4 specifications as they become available.

Logical Volume Manager

OSF/1 provides a logical volume manager, which allows multiple physical disk drives to be seen as one logical disk drive. In today's commercial environment this feature is useful for applications utilizing large databases, in which a single file can be larger than any single physical disk in the system.

The OSF/1 logical volume manager also supports disk mirroring, in which multiple copies of files are automatically maintained on different physical disks. Disk mirroring protects data integrity in the face of hardware failures. It also provides high availability of data for increased performance in commercial applications by fetching the "nearest" record on a read.

UI/USL have announced that they are partnering with Veritas to provide similar capability.

Real Time

OSF/1, as well as SVR4, must await the emergence of fixed standards for fully functional real-time systems before either can truly embody the features that will be required for a standards-oriented, open, real-time system. Although neither SVR4 nor OSF/1 is designed as an optimized real-time system, each provides real-time features such as POSIX high-resolution timers.

OSF/1's approach of layering subsystems on the Mach kernel will make it easy to adapt OSF/1 to real-time applications in the future.

SVR4 provides a scheduler switch architecture and pre-emption points within the kernel, allowing a certain degree of user-controlled scheduling.

Program Management

The OSF/1 operating system provides a rich set of features for managing the program execution environment and for increasing program performance. Some of these features, formerly bound to the operating system kernel, have been moved into user space and are easily customizable. These features include:

- Support for shared libraries, including application libraries

- Support for load-time object module relocation

- Support for object module format independence

- A set of callable, user space loader interfaces

OSF/1 supports both relocatable and absolute shared libraries. With dynamically loaded shared libraries, each application no longer needs to contain its own private copy of the routines in the library. This provides several advantages over statically linked libraries. Because the library code is shared, applications are smaller, use less disk space, and provide for more efficient utilization of main memory. Because applications do not require relinking after modification to a shared library, software vendors can distribute shared libraries as an update without affecting existing installed applications.

The OSF/1 program loader also can resolve an object module's external references at load time rather than just at link time as in some traditional systems. The loader supports position independent code which is compiled and executed correctly regardless of its location in memory.

The OSF/1 program loader resides in user space, maintaining the simplicity of the operating system's modular kernel while supporting enhanced program loading functions. The program loader was designed to handle multiple object file formats. Its clean separation of format-independent and format-dependent parts, as well as the separation of machine-independent and machine-dependent code, makes extending the loader for new formats a straightforward process. As delivered by OSF, the OSF/1 program loader supports COFF and OSF/ROSE (an evolution of the Carnegie Mellon University Mach-O format). A system vendor can extend the loader to identify other formats, thereby providing backward binary compatibility with that vendor's existing installed format base.

In addition to loading programs and libraries, the OSF/1 loader provides a fully documented programming interface. Programs can use the loader to call in program modules and unload them as needed. This facility is particularly useful for larger applications such as computer aided design or artificial intelligence programs which may face memory constraints or which may need to construct object code on the fly.

SVR4 provides support for shared libraries, dynamic linking and loading of program modules, and position independent code and therefore has similar capabilities to OSF/1 in that regard. The SVR4 program loader is capable of loading either COFF or ELF (Extensible Linking Format) but is not extensible to load other formats.

SVR4 provides a multi-window, menu-driven interface for alpha-numeric terminals called Framed Access Command Environment (FACE). FACE provides a "user friendly" command environment for end users. OSF/1 has no offering in this area and none is planned. The Open Software Foundation is concentrating on newer technologies associated with graphical user interfaces (for example, Motif). However, various licensees of OSF/1 provide similar alpha-numeric interface capabilities as part of their value-add.

Dynamic Configuration

OSF/1 supports dynamic linking and loading (that is, loading while the operating system is running) of kernel modules for file systems, networking protocols, device drivers, pseudo device drivers, STREAMS modules and drivers, and user space code. OSF/1 can dynamically load kernel modules at run time, making it unnecessary to reboot the system to add these modules to the system's configuration database. For software vendors, this feature presents an opportunity to market kernel subsystems that can be installed and configured in an easy and consistent manner.

SVR4 does not support dynamically loadable kernel modules.

General Open Systems Comparison

Compatibility

Adherence to standards is important as a means of enabling application portability between systems. The OSF/1 operating system complies with all relevant industry standards and specifications including:

- ANSI C
- FIPS 151-1
- POSIX 1003.1-1988
- X/Open Portability Guide Issue 3.

OSF/1 also complies with the Programming Interfaces Volume of the OSF Applications Environment Specification (AES), the multivolume publication that defines the interfaces needed to develop portable applications for an open systems environment. The AES is a comprehensive specification for the entire open environment: from the user interface to networking. The primary purpose of the AES is to provide a common definition of application interfaces that both systems providers and systems users can rely on in the development of portable applications. Furthermore, the AES is OSF's commitment to forward compatibility with industry standards over time.

System V Release 4 complies with AT&T's System V Interface Definition (SVID) Issue 3 for the System V operating system and also supports the ANSI C, POSIX and XPG3 specifications. Both organizations have promised to conform to XPG4 when it is published. Since both operating systems claim compliance with the same set of standards and specifications, the end user can be assured that both new and existing applications written to these standards will run on either operating system.

In addition, OSF/1 supports elements of the IEEE draft POSIX 1003.4 specification, including timers and threads implementations. The OSF/1 threads implementation conforms to the POSIX 1003.4a Pthreads draft standard. USL has indicated that it has no plans to support the POSIX threads standard in System V Release 4.

In addition to standards conformance, OSF/1 also merges the Berkeley Software Distribution and System V commands and libraries to provide an operating system interface compatible with either BSD or System V. Developers of software, as well as end users, that are familiar with either system will feel immediately at home with the OSF/1 operating system.

SVR4 provides a merge of selected 4.3BSD, Sun/OS, System V, and Xenix commands. The level of completeness of this merge is unclear.

Portability/Scalability of the Operating System

The OSF/1 system is portable and scalable. Its Mach kernel has run on platforms ranging from PCs to supercomputers. In a demonstration of its portability and scalability, OSF provides on the OSF/1 release tape three reference implementations and three vendor contributed ports of the OSF/1 operating system. The reference platforms include an Intel 80386-based machine (CISC), a DECstation-3100 MIPS-based machine (RISC), and Encore's multiprocessor supermini-computer (National Semiconductor chip). Vendors have contributed ports for distribution on the OSF tape for machines based on the Motorola 68030 (Hewlett Packard), Fairchild Clipper (Intergraph), and Intel i860 chips (Intel).

In addition, vendors such as IBM, Intel, Encore Computer Corporation, Digital Equipment Corporation, Hewlett-Packard/Apollo, Intergraph, Siemens/Nixdorf Information Systems, Groupe Bull, Hitachi, and others have adapted the OSF/1 operating system to a wide variety of platforms in the OSF Portability Lab.

OSF/1 will support companies' diverse computer systems, and it will allow those companies to maintain their software environment when they upgrade their hardware.

SVR4 also has been ported to architectures ranging in size from PCs to supercomputers. With the exception of multiprocessing platforms, the portability and scalability of the two operating systems are similar in this regard.

Applications Portability

The portability of applications is important to end users who wish to protect the investments they've made in software. Hardware vendors are interested in portable applications in order to have a wide range of applications available for their platforms, making them more attractive to end users. Independent software vendors are interested in portability in order to have the widest target market for their applications without the need to maintain multiple hardware-specific sources. OSF/1 provides compatibility features to satisfy all of these constituencies.

For independent software vendors and end users, OSF/1 can execute a large variety of applications including:

- System V applications written to the System V Interface Definition Issue 2 (base and kernel extensions)

- 4.3 BSD applications

- Applications written to the POSIX 1003.1 and XPG3 specifications.

Applications Portability Through ANDF

OSF is further addressing applications portability through its Architecture-Neutral Distribution Format (ANDF). The OSF is acquiring technologies for the ANDF through the RFT process. The ANDF will provide an intermediate format (analogous to an intermediate file out of a compiler) that can be used across all platforms. Therefore, a software vendor will be able to distribute one shrink-wrapped version of an application which will run on any hardware that supports the ANDF. End users will be able to purchase the application in this intermediate format and install it using an installer/translator provided by their system vendor.

Consequently, software vendors needn't port their applications to various processor types, as they would if they employed an Application Binary Interface (ABI) — an operating system and processor-dependent approach to software distribution. The ANDF doesn't preclude the use of ABIs, however. An existing ABI can be used to develop an installer/translator that could serve all platforms conforming to the ABI.

The ANDF approach clearly benefits software developers and end users: the developers can maintain one copy of source code and needn't port applications to a plethora of platforms, and users are assured a wide selection of off-the-shelf software, no matter what ANDF-compliant hardware they choose to buy. But ANDF benefits systems vendors as well. Traditionally, systems vendors have had to rely on software vendors' willingness to port existing applications to the hardware vendors' new platforms. ANDF reduces this interdependence. When a system vendor introduces a new hardware architecture, the vendor need only write another ANDF installer to ensure the new architecture will run a multitude of off-the-shelf applications.

USL's approach to applications portability will apparently rely on ABIs, which requires applications developers to recompile their source code for each of their targeted architectures. USL claims to have, or have in development, ABIs for several processors. The ABI approach does not provide the industry with the freedom to pursue hardware architecture innovations and still leverage shrink-wrap applications.

Networking and Interoperability

The networking capabilities of OSF/1 give developers compatibility with current applications, the ability to take advantage of multiprocessor systems for high performance, and a high-level programming interface for the creation of portable network applications.

The OSF/1 system includes fully parallelized versions of the widely used network protocols and frameworks including the Internet protocols; the BSD Sockets interface, enhanced to include features from 4.4BSD; a System V-compatible STREAMS framework; and an NFS-compatible distributed file system. New and existing network applications running on OSF/1 can take advantage of the system's inherent support for multiprocessing and the parallelization of the STREAMS and Sockets frameworks to achieve high performance levels.

OSF/1 supports the TCP/IP Internet protocol family, including the most recent "Reno" release and Tahoe changes for the Berkeley Internet facilities. OSF/1 also supports the IEEE 802.3 Ethernet protocol and Serial Line Interface Protocol (SLIP).

SVR4 supplies the Internet protocols, STREAMS, and NFS although Internet is provided as an extra cost option. SLIP does not appear in their literature as supported. None of the SVR4 networking subsystems are parallelized for concurrent operation on multiprocessor hardware.

The OSF/1 operating system also provides a parallelized X/Open Transport Interface (XTI). As specified in the XPG3 Networking Guide, XTI is a vendor-neutral application programming interface for network applications. Using XTI, developers can write network applications that are independent of the underlying transport mechanism. The XTI implementation in OSF/1 provides a path to either the Sockets or STREAMS frameworks through a library of routines for compatibility with protocol families using either framework. XTI is the preferred methodology for software vendors wishing to write portable network applications. XTI is part of the OSF Application Environment Specification. The OSF/1 XTI facility provides backward compatibility with applications written for AT&T's Transport Layer Interface (TLI).

TLI, which was first introduced in SVR3, is supported in SVR4. X/Open based XTI on TLI, but added some additional functionality in the areas of error codes and event notification. Although TLI includes most of XTI, USL does not claim full XTI compatibility in SVR4 because of these extensions.

The Open Software Foundation is further addressing interoperability in distributed, heterogeneous computing environments through its Distributed Computing Environment (DCE), which is operating-system and network independent. The

DCE will provide functions such as remote procedure call, time and naming services, security, a distributed file system, and other services.

The UI/USL approach to providing these required services for distributed computing is a plan to add more functionality to the operating system itself. This will add to the complexity of an already overly complex system.

Business Case

Overview

Many of the benefits of OSF/1 result from the structure of the Open Software Foundation itself. OSF is a nonprofit organization formed by sponsors Apollo (now a subsidiary of Hewlett-Packard), Digital, Groupe Bull, Hewlett-Packard, Hitachi, IBM, Philips, and Nixdorf and Siemens (now SNI).

OSF membership now includes more than 250 systems manufacturers, software developers, end users, and academic and research organizations.

OSF's offerings are specifications, implementations, and validation technology, not just of an operating system, but of a complete open systems software environment. Technologies are solicited and evaluated through an open process, often including a Request for Technology (RFT). The resulting decisions reflect the requirements of the membership; decisions are not controlled by any one systems manufacturer. Some of the technologies resulting from the RFT process include the Motif graphical user interface, the Distributed Computing Environment (DCE), and two new technologies currently being evaluated, the Architecture-Neutral Distribution Format (ANDF), and the Distributed Management Environment (DME).

In contrast, Unix International develops the System V road map, a set of recommendations for the evolution of System V, and presents these requirements to UNIX System Labs, an internal AT&T development organization for System V. USL evaluates these requirements and determines which features and functions will be developed for System V; the final decisions are made by USL. There is no mechanism for incorporating "best in industry" technologies; all development is apparently designed and controlled by USL.

Finally, OSF provides to its members early and equal access to development code under its snapshot program and portability lab. Software and system vendors needn't rely on abstract specifications when they develop applications for future OSF releases; they can work with the actual code as it is being developed, providing a significant advantage in getting products to market early.

Pricing

OSF is committed to fair and equitable licensing. An OSF/1 source license with redistribution rights costs $50,000 — one half that of SVR4, although OSF/1 licensees must have a System V.2 (or later) license from AT&T. Even with the V.3 licensing fee, which is the most common, OSF/1's total cost is comparable to SVR4 for small systems and roughly one-third less for large systems. Moreover, unlike the complex licensing scheme for SVR4, the OSF/1 license fee is not dependent on system revenue or system software costs. An OSF/1 license is available to OSF members and nonmembers alike at the same cost. Licensees of OSF/1 receive not only the base operating system but also all additional facilities such as internationalization, security, and networking support. These features must be purchased separately for SVR4.

Open Environment — Not Just An Operating System

OSF/1 is part of the Open Software Foundation's complete open systems environment. To enable systems and software to work together in such an environment, OSF's Application Environment Specification defines stable, consistent application-level interfaces for the operating system as well as for user environment services, networking services, graphics services, database management services, and programming languages. By means of the AES, the Open Software Foundation allows users to select the technology and functionality they need, and users can be assured that the AES-compliant technologies they choose are smoothly integrated.

OSF's open systems environment now includes OSF/1 plus these offerings:

- The widely accepted OSF/Motif graphical user interface, which offers users and programmers a simple way to standardize application presentation. OSF/Motif is consistent with popular windowing systems on PCs as it offers the style of Presentation Manager. OSF/Motif is layered on the MIT X Window System graphics tools.

- The Distributed Computing Environment (DCE), which promotes interoperability in heterogeneous computing environments. DCE provides operating system and network-independent distributed computing services, like remote procedure call, naming service, time service, security service, threads service, distributed file system, diskless support, and MS-DOS file and printer support.

OSF plans enhanced system administration features and has issued a Request for Technology for its Distributed Management Environment (DME). OSF/1 now provides the 4.3 Berkeley system administration base along with System V accounting commands. The DME will embody emerging POSIX 1003.7 standards as well as those from the X/Open Working Group on System Administration.

The Open Look graphical user interface is available with SVR4. Distributed computing is provided through Sun Microsystems' ONC and the AT&T RFS file system, neither of which address the need for distributed services in multivendor computing environments.

OSF Business Advantages

OSF & OSF/1	UI & SVR4
OSF/1 has a committed plan; it includes all the functionality in the 5-year road-map for SVR4	System V Roadmap is a 5-year require-ments document, not a plan
OSF/1 is industry owned: • OSF is a broad-based industry con-stituency • OSF president reports to OSF Board of Directors • OSF has neutral decision making by OSF staff and members	System V is controlled by USL: • UNIX International is a supplier/cus-tomer collaborative (user group) • USL president reports to AT&T • USL makes the final decision on Sys-tem V.4 technologies
OSF/1 provides vendors significant economies that can be passed on to end users: • Source licenses up to 30% less than System V.4 • Simplified licensing structure - fixed fee for each binary copy with stan-dard volume discounts. B1 security, internationalization, TCP/IP, and NFS compatibility bundled. • Microkernel strategy could eventually eliminate cost of System V license now required for OSF/1 • RFT process acquires technology at very competitive prices due to poten-tial large size of OSF market; the Mach kernel was licensed from Car-negie Mellon Univ. on a no-cost basis. • RFT process is an exhaustive, open, neutral, fair process of selecting the technology that best meets market and industry needs with regard to Open Systems - ensuring portability and interoperability between UNIX and non-UNIX systems.	System V.4 licenses are structured in terms of a percentage of system revenue or system software costs: • Complex licensing structure with binary license fee based on target list price of machine. B2 security and internationalization (mid 91) TCP/IP, and NFS are licensed separately

OSF Technology Advantages

OSF & OSF/1	UI & SVR4
OSF/1 provides the benefits of a modern architecture with the Mach kernel (System V.5 today!) • OSF/1 was originally designed for and supports Symmetric Multiprocessing (SMP) and is a better platform in terms of performance scalability. • Microkernel strategy will provide support for highly customizable, special purpose, distributed servers (e.g. print, file, and networking). Also will provide multiple O/S personalities and a foundation for B3 security.	V.4 forestalls an inevitable System V redesign which is implied by the System V Roadmap. This redesign is sometimes referred to as System V.5 • Full SMP is not available until mid-1992, according to the 9/90 AT&T announcement. • The current System V kernel is too large to permit implementation of full B3 security.
OSF provides more than just an operating system. • Distributed Computing Environment - Gartner predicts DCE will be de facto standard for client/server computing by 1993. • Graphical User Interface - Motif closes gap between UNIX and PC worlds by offering a Presentation Manager style of behavior. Motif is operating system independent and can be used on both open and proprietary systems. • Access to "shrink wrapped" software - OSF's Architecture Neutral Distribution Format (ANDF) represents a pathway to "true" shrink-wrapped UNIX software. It will provide a single intermediate form that can go to end users for any supported computer platform. ANDF is planned for release in 4Q91. • DME - a vendor neutral Distributed Management Environment is now in the RFT phase. DME will greatly reduce the complexity and cost system administrators face in managing systems from various vendors.	USL's initial development efforts focus on the operating system. • Even UI members have endorsed DCE: System V does not address distributed computing (Network Computing Plus) until 1994 or beyond. • OPEN LOOK, while based on X Windows, is not consistent with PC window systems. It perpetuates the separation of the PC and UNIX worlds. • System V.4 offers a partial solution via its Application Binary Interface (ABI). However, a different application version for each hardware architecture is still required.

Future Path

OSF/1 provides features like multiprocessing today. For the future, it offers a path to an open, modular, extensible architecture and a path to B3-level security features. Ultimately, a microkernel, free of AT&T licensing requirements, could provide essential functionality, such as virtual memory management, secure interprocess communication, scheduling, and device support. Specialized server processes executing in user space could deliver additional required operating system functionality.

OSF/1's Mach base permits a steady evolution toward the microkernel goal, ensuring that users, systems vendors, and software developers can take advantage of added functionality without compromising the existing software base and end-user investments.

Conclusion

OSF/1 is the technologically and economically superior choice for an open system operating environment for the '90s and beyond. It complies with standards as they evolve, is compatible with earlier software, and is based on proven technology. Yet it is also innovative and positioned for a smooth evolution toward a new structure to meet future application requirements. The OSF/1 architecture supports improved extensibility that facilitates the addition of vendor-created value-added enhancements and technologies arising from the open process.

ADDENDUM

OSF/1 vs. SVR4 Feature Comparison

OSF/1 is a UNIX-like operating system in which OSF's open process was used to determine the included technology. OSF/1 represents a full featured UNIX operating system that has been restructured to provide functionality and a growth path beyond what is available with traditional UNIX implementations.

In addition to the features and functions that the market expects of a UNIX-based operating system, OSF/1 provides the features and functions required by the next generation of hardware and software products.

The following table compares the features of the OSF/1 operating system with System V Release 4, in regard to conformance with POSIX 1003.1, ANSI C and X/Open Portability Guide Issue 3.

The majority of the "feature set" items were taken from the October 11, 1988 draft of the Technical Reference Manual, UNIX System V and Open System Standards.

Feature Set Comparison

Feature Set	Accepted Industry Standards (Existing Specifications)			Operating Systems Comparison To Standards	
	POSIX	ANSI C	XPG3	SVR4	OSF/1
Error Codes & Conditions	●		●	●	●
Environment Description	●		●	●	●
Process Execution & Control	●		●	●	●
Process Status & Resources	●		●	●	●
File-Systems & Directories	●		●	●	●
File & Device Input/Output	●		●	●	●
Standard Input/Output		●	●	●	●
Locale & Character Routines		●	●	●	●
String Handling Routines		●	●	●	●
Formatted Input/Output		●	●	●	●
Common Library Routines		●	●	●	●
Mathematical Functions		●	●	●	●
Multi-Tasking Coordination			●	●	●
Software Development Tools			●	●	●
Basic Utilities			●	●	●
Advanced Utilities			●	●	●
Administrative Services			●	●	●
Character Terminal Interface			●	●	●
Transport Layer Interface			●	●	●
Distributed File System				●	●
Virtual Memory Services				●	●
Xenix Compatibility				●	
B1 Security Functionality					●
Graphical User Interface				●	●
Real-Time Services				●	**
Remote Procedure Call				●	*
Presentation Manager				●	*
Extended Terminal Interface				●	
Mach Foundation					●
Extensible Loader					●
Symmetric Multiprocessing					●
Threads					●
Logical Volume Manager					●

* These components plus other features are addressed in the DCE offering.
** Equivalent or better performance

Features Comparison Matrix

Feature	OSF/1	V.4.0
"Standards"		
POSIX 1003.1	Y	Y
POSIX 1003.4 draft		
Pthreads	Y	N
Timers	Y	Y
ANSI X3J11 C	Y	Y
FIPS 151-1	Y	Y
XPG3 base	Y	Y
XPG3 XTI	Y	N (TLI)
XPG3 extensions beyond base	N	N
XPG3 Source Brand	Y	Y
SVID Issue 2 base	Y	Y (Issue 3)
SVID Issue 2 kernel extensions	Y	Y (Issue 3)
msg queues, semaphores, sh. mem.,		
acct, chroot, nice, plock, profil, ptrace		
SVID Issue 2 STREAMS services	Y	Y (Issue 3)
getmsg, putmsg, poll		
SVID Issue 3	N	Y
4.3 BSD		
"fast file system"	Y	Y
source compatibility	Y	"High degree"
cshell	Y	Y
commands	Y	some
system calls	Y	some
long filenames	Y	Y
sockets API	Y	Y
sockets framework	Y	N
symbolic links	Y	Y
job control	Y	Y
ptys	Y	Y
concurrent groups	Y	Y
mapped files: mmap()	Y	Y
BCS/ABI support	N	various
Applications Environment	Y	N
Specification (AES) compliance		
Validation Suite	Y	Y
File Systems		
Virtual File System	Y	Y
System V	Y	Y
UFS	Y	Y
Network File System (NFS) Version 2 compat.	Y	Y
/proc filesystem	N	Y

Feature	OSF/1	V.4.0
Networking		
STREAMS Framework	Y	Y
Sockets Framework	Y (4.3+4.4)	Y (4.3 only)
XTI XPG3	Y	N
TLI	Y	Y
DARPA protocols (TCP,IP,UDP,ICMP, ARP)	Y	Y (extra cost)
TCP/IP Performance improvements	Y	Y (extra cost)
Serial line Internet Protocol (SLIP)	Y	N
(with optional header compression)		
uucp	Y	Y
Diskless support	N (DCE)	Y
Program Management		
COFF	Y	Y
ELF	(possible	Y
	via loader	
	switch)	
OSF/ROSE	Y	N
PIC	Y	Y
Dynamic shared libraries	Y	Y
Dynamic linking	Y	Y
Demand loading	Y	Y
Object File Format Independence	Y	N
Extensible Loader	Y	N
Tools	Y	Y
Kernel Features		
Symmetric MP	Y	N
MP Set Scheduling	Y	N
Parallelized		
NFS-compatible file system	Y	N
UFS	Y	N
VFS	Y	N
VM subsystem	Y	N
TCP/IP	Y	N
STREAMS framework	Y	N
Sockets framework	Y	N
Real time features		
POSIX high resolution timers	Y	Y
scheduler switch architecture	Y	Y
preemptible kernel	N	preemption pts.
user-controlled scheduling	N	Y
Dynamically loadable kernel modules		
file systems	Y	N

Feature	OSF/1	V.4.0
networking protocols	Y	N
device drivers	Y	N
pseudo device drivers	Y	N
STREAMS modules/drivers	Y	N
Kernel debugging and performance measurement	Y	Y
ddi/dki	Y	Y
Terminal Handling		
terminfo	Y	Y
curses	Y	Y
STREAMS tty subsystem	N (Rel. 1.1)	Y
FACE/FMLI	N	Y
Printing		
BSD lp support	Y	Y
Native Language Support		
Eight-bit clean commands	Y	Y
Multi-byte support	Y	Y
Collating sequence	Y	Y
Message catalogs	Y	Y
Message handling facilities	Y	Y
Localization (setlocale, locale def)	Y	Y
Other XPG3 base features	Y	Y
Japanese Language Support	Y	MNLS
Security		
Full C2-level security features	Y	N (MLS)
Full B1 level security features	Y	N (MLS)
Full B2-level security features	N	N (SVR4 ES)
B2/B3 features		
access control lists	Y	N (SVR4 ES)
DAC	Y	N (SVR4 ES)
least privilege	Y	N (SVR4 ES)
trusted facility mgmt.	Y	N (SVR4 ES)
Advanced Features		
Tasks and Threads	Y	N
External pager capability	Y	N
Portable VM	Y	Y
Network transparent IPC	Y	N
Scheduling/CPU control	Y	N

Feature	OSF/1	V.4.0
System Administration		
System Administration		
Berkeley system admin base	Y	N
System V system admin base	N (acct. only)	Y
Logical volume management	Y	N
Disk mirroring	Y	N
Menu-driven	N	Y
Disk quotas	Y	Y
Dynamic configuration	Y	N
Software installation & change control tools	Y	Y
Validation and Testing		
Functional & system tests	Y	N
Validation suite	Y	Y
Documentation		
Porting guide	Y	N
Internals documentation	Y	N
Component specs. for AES	Y	SVID
Commands & system call reference	Y	Y
Extensive indexes	Y	N
Release notes	Y	Y
Validation	Y	Y
On-line and hardcopy	Y	Y